Endoi

The Spirit of God that's within Prophet John Veal's pen has breathed a prophetic masterpiece! *Supernaturally Prophetic* is a great book for prophetic training. Practical, applicable, and impactful is this prophetic work. Every generation is blessed to have genuine prophetic voices in the midst of them, and we are blessed with Prophet John Veal. I endorse this book and its contents. Go pick it up!

DETRICK LAMONT GASKINS
Author of *From the Lord Comes Deliverance*
and *Restoring Regions*

I highly recommend Prophet John Veal's book *Supernaturally Prophetic* as your prophetic guide book, for it brings greater awareness and clarity for prophets and prophetic people!

This book allows you to glean and learn from someone with years of acquired experience and knowledge in this realm of supernatural gifting and positioning in terms of office!

Prophet Veal will take you on a profound course of learning as you read this book, which highlights his journey as a true prophet of the Lord! *Get the book* and let it help you become prophetically astute!

SHARON RUFF PETERS
Author of *Teach Me to Pray, Who Hurt the Church, Thoughts of the Morning, 31 Days of Divine Thinking, The 3F's That Make for a Successful Christian,* and *Help for the Help Meet*

Prophet Veal really cracks the seals off of the prophetic in his book *Supernaturally Prophetic*. This book will educate you, equip you, and excite you. Every young prophet and/or those who are looking to stir up the prophetic gift in their life need to get a copy. The oil on this word will truly seep into the depths of your spirit as you feast on its contents.

JOSHUA BOTELLO
Author of *The Samson Code, From Here to There, My Cup Overfloweth*, and *Diaries of a Soilshaker*

In this dynamic book *Supernaturally Prophetic*, John Veal shares a wealth of experience and personal supernatural and prophetic encounters with God. This book is fully loaded with answers to tough questions concerning prophecy, prophets, and the prophetic ministry in the twenty-first century. He challenges the reader to break the fear of the prophetic and move in the realm of boldness, confidence and assurance in hearing, obeying and responding to the voice of God. *Supernaturally Prophetic* is not just a book on the prophetic but has the potency to activate the supernatural gift of faith to prophesy that will bring healing, deliverance, transformation, and tremendous breakthroughs.

John Veal is a modern-day accurate prophet and teacher called to bring reformation, education, and impartation in the Body of Christ in the areas of the prophetic, spiritual warfare, and deliverance. He has written a comprehensive study guide that will educate, equip, activate, upgrade, and assist contemporary prophets, prophetic leadership, and believers in the things of the Spirit. The personal supernatural testimonies and revelation contained on these pages by John Veal will make you laugh, cry, and relate to his prophetic process and the making of a prophet.

I highly recommend this literature for anyone who has a desire to grow in their relationship with the Father and in the prophetic gift, call, and ministry. After finishing this book, you will feel empowered, refreshed, equipped, and most of all *Supernaturally Prophetic!*

HAKEEM COLLINS
Champions International
Author of *Born to Prophesy, Heaven Declares, Prophetic Breakthrough,* and *Command Your Healing*

Our generation will prophesy! *Supernaturally Prophetic* is a wonderful, practical, and very timely prophetic publication. Never before in history has the Church so needed the prophets of God to speak up and to speak clearly. This book does that and it tells you how to do it, with practical examples and inspiring, heartwarming personal experiences, John Veal carries the heart of the prophetic for this generation and many to come. This book will add fuel to your prophetic fire. The world needs this message, and every person alive needs this book!

WALTER V. WILLIAMS
Worship Leader
Author of *Lifestyle Worship*

John Veal has with mastery, skill, and experience written *Supernaturally Prophetic.* This book is broken into five books like the book of Psalms. That is intriguing to me as the psalms speak of who God is just like John is speaking to who and what the prophetic is. With Scripture and prophetic experiences, John proves the validity of the prophetic in the twenty-first-century Church. He describes what the prophetic is, how it operates, and how to embrace it. I love this book. Thank you for giving understanding to the prophetic process—great job, Prophet John Veal.

Javon Rahman Bertrand
Author of *The Biography of Prophets*

Prophet John Veal is a prophet who carries the wisdom of God in the earth and represents the office of the prophet with boldness, clarity, and authority. This book is a must-read for all generations. There is a fresh anointing that flows through every page and provides readers with information as well as an impartation. You will receive revelation and will be eager to go after God in a new way. This book will serve as a resource guide that is much needed like never before.

Supernaturally Prophetic will stir you, activate you, train you, and release you to hear God for yourself. I highly recommend this book and encourage you to use it as a resource for prophetic training.

Sophia Ruffin
Author of *From Point Guard to Prophet*
and *Set Free and Delivered*
SophiaRuffin.com

In 1987, I was called into the prophetic ministry. At that time, there were few books on how to function in prophetic ministry, and revelation concerning the prophetic office was nearly non-existent. Since then, we have had a myriad of books on the prophetic office and ministry. But very few contain practical and biblical instructions. That has led to confusion regarding the prophetic office and ministry. Today, we have many men and women claiming to be prophets who are not, and many false or inaccurate prophetic words being given. Some have tried to address those issues. But to date, few, apart from my friend John Veal in his book *Supernaturally Prophetic*, provide clear instruction, guidance, and correction. I am grateful for his practical teaching and instruction in *Supernaturally Prophetic*, especially his teaching and wisdom on prophetic therapy. And I find his book to be on par with those great books I have read on the prophetic office and ministry.

SCOTT WALLIS
Prophet and author of *Entering the School of the Prophets, Plugging into the Spirit of Prophecy,* and *How to Know If Your Prophecy Is Really From God*

It is with great honor and privilege that I wholeheartedly recommend this practical and sharp tool in the hands of the Lord to the prophetic movement and Body of Christ. Writing out of both experience and revelation, John Veal gives profound keys and wisdom regarding how to operate in authentic prophetic ministry and also warns of the potential dangers of moving in prophecy.

John Veal is a trusted prophetic father to this generation and I'm greatly encouraged that God is now calling him to speak up and out about prophetic ministry. If you are ready to grow in your prophetic gifts and be given wisdom and insight as you mature, start reading now. You will not be disappointed!

JEREMIAH JOHNSON
Founder of Jeremiah Johnson Ministries
Founder and Elder at Heart of the Father Ministry
Author of *I See A New Prophetic Generation* and *The Micaiah Company: A Prophetic Reformation*

SUPERNATURALLY
PROPHETIC

SUPERNATURALLY PROPHETIC

A PRACTICAL GUIDE FOR PROPHETS AND PROPHETIC PEOPLE

JOHN VEAL

DESTINY IMAGE® PUBLISHERS, INC.

P.O. Box 310, Shippensburg, PA 17257-0310

"Promoting Inspired Lives."

This book and all other Destiny Image and Destiny Image Fiction books are available at Christian bookstores and distributors worldwide.

Cover design by Eileen Rockwell
Interior design by Terry Clifton

For more information on foreign distributors, call 717-532-3040.

Reach us on the Internet: www.destinyimage.com.

ISBN 13 TP: 978-0-7684-4633-3
ISBN 13 eBook: 978-0-7684-4634-0
ISBN 13 HC: 978-0-7684-4636-4
ISBN 13 LP: 978-0-7684-4635-7

Previously Published ISBN: 978-0-9993376-0-8

For Worldwide Distribution, Printed in the U.S.A.
1 2 3 4 5 6 7 8 / 22 21 20 19 18

Acknowledgments

First, I have to give thanks to my *Lord and Savior, Jesus Christ*. If it weren't for Him, this book would not have been written. His testimony is the spirit of prophecy. Lord, you are the love of my life! Thank you for keeping me thus far.

To my rib and better half, my wife, *Elisa Veal*: God supernaturally showed me that you were to be my spouse way back in grammar school. However, you didn't see it until much later in life. You truly have been my support system, my confidant, comrade, and lover since our wedding day. You're one of the strongest women I've ever met. I've watched you mature into the world's greatest mother to our three little girls. You are the epitome of a virtuous woman as described in Proverbs 31. Sometimes, I have to pinch myself when I see you sleeping next to me. I'm so blessed to have you as my companion for life. I truly believe that one of the reasons God saved me was to save you, too! Love you forever, honey!

To my oldest daughter, *Jennifer:* You are truly called as a prophetess to the nations! You are our first born after years of unsuccessful attempts to have a child. One day, while your mom and I were watching you on an ultrasound monitor, I heard the Lord say, "I'm in here with her." When you finally arrived, it was love at first sight, the type of love that only parents can truly know.

From that day forward, I knew that you were called to greatness. I love you, Jen Jen!

To my middle daughter, *Jessica:* You are the most compassionate of our three children; you always think of others before yourself. I believe that compassion is one of your greatest strengths; never lose it! Don't ever think that it's a weakness. You have brought me extreme joy since the day you were born. Out of all our children, you were the only one that cried at birth. My heart melted as you smiled at me only hours later. You are beautiful inside and out. I am so proud of you and know that the Lord will use you greatly in life. Always remember that what you make happen for others, God will make happen for you. I love you, Tex Mex!

To my youngest daughter, *Jayla:* You are the comedian of the family; you bring joy and laughter to every situation in which you find yourself. I call you "the last of the Mohicans" because you came when your mother and I thought we were done having children. You were not an accident but were planned for with love. Various people prophesied about you, so we had to be obedient. You have been an absolute treasure ever since your birth. I'm so glad that we listened to the Lord! He told me that you were here for His purposes. Always remember that! I love you, Jay Bird!

To my spiritual mother, *Ruth Brown*: Your love and investment in me was immense. All the days of fussing at me were overshadowed by the genuine concern you displayed. You were as loving as you were tough. The prophetic words that you spoke over me are still coming to pass as I am writing this. For that and so much more, I am truly grateful. I can still remember you "making" me prophesy to you, telling me that it was training. You were right. You left me way too soon, but I know that you are currently enjoying your heavenly reward. I miss you every day! I love you, Mother Ruthie!

To my mother, *Beverly E. Veal*, and my biological father, *Andre L. Dunigan*: I thank you both for bringing me into this world. You were both so young when I was born, yet you took on the responsibility of raising a child. I truly wish that you were still here. You left us way too soon, but I know that you're with our heavenly Father. Love you! See you later!

To my apostle, *John Eckhardt*: You have inspired me beyond what words can express. Your humility, intelligence, impartations, compassion, and experience have greatly benefited me. I learn from you on a daily basis. The talks we've had always leave me feeling refreshed and ready to take on the rigors of ministry. Thank you for being a leader whom I can look up to, full of wisdom and integrity. You demonstrate such graciousness by your willingness to share your platform and influence with others. You model a wonderful gift of mercy that I want to emulate. I'm so thankful for the day the Lord told me to reach out to you. My life has been the better for it. Thank you for being my spiritual father. Love you to life!

Special thanks to:

Bishop Monroe Mullins: Thank you for ordaining me into ministry. You listened to God and sent me out. I will never forget you or what you did for me. I truly appreciate you.

Prophet Darryl and Prophetess Jacqueline Washington: Thank you for being my closest friends for the last twenty-one years and for helping to lead me back to Jesus Christ. You both have always been a listening ear for me. Love you, Prophetic Judge!

Bishop Randy Horn: Thank you for being the first pastor to make the Word come alive for my wife and me. You gave us both a very solid foundation in the Bible that still serves us well. I will always love and appreciate you.

Apostle Clifford and Lady Darlyn Turner: Thank you for prophetically speaking my ministry into life way back in 1999. I have never been quite the same since that day. I appreciate how you always encourage my service for the King. You and the Liberty Temple family are truly an inspiration to me.

Pastor Walter V. Williams: Thanks for being more than just a partner in ministry. You've been a great friend. I appreciate all you do for me personally and for our church. Love you to life!

Apostle Lajun and Prophetess Valora Cole: Thank you for inspiring and encouraging me in my suddenly season! I am truly grateful for our friendship. You guys are awesome!

Joseph Crofton: Thanks for being there for me throughout the years. You were there for some of my happiest moments and the darkest ones. You are a trusted friend.

Amber McAfee-Barnes: Thanks so much for helping to get me started on this book! Your words challenged and pushed me. Love you to life!

I also would like to thank the following ministries and people for their support: my entire Enduring Faith Christian Center family (past, present, and future), Liberty Temple of Chicago and Waukegan, Crusaders Church, Destined To Win Christian

Center, Power and Authority Church, Jeffery and Rhonda Veal, Earl and Bertha Rowe, Alicia and Damon Johnson, Andrais and Kairi Thornton, Joseph and Sharon Rowe, Carmolita Hubbard, Lamar Baker, Helen S. Wells, Lauren Wells, Jeffery W. Veal II, Sherman and Vicki White, Pamela Taylor, Sheanon Mays, Shirene Anderson, Sheraine Lathon, Thomas and Esther Johnson, Laron Matthews, Deland John and Kisia Fells-Coleman, Kelvin and Tonya Easter, Ryan LeStrange, Joshua and Marshkia Botello, Darrell and Venessa Yarber, Scott Wallis, Theresa Harvard Johnson, Sue Branch, Yvonne Lovelady, Trey and Jasmine Fisher, Ebony Murrell, Sophia Ruffin, Sharon R. Peters, Nina-Marie Leslie, Shan E. Davis, Bernadette Washington, Theresa Harvard Johnson, and a host of others, far too many to name.

Contents

Foreword 1

Introduction 5

PART I All Can Prophesy 9

CHAPTER 1 My Supernatural Beginnings 11

CHAPTER 2 What Is Prophecy? 23

CHAPTER 3 You Are Inherently Prophetic! 27

PART II Prophecy 101 43

CHAPTER 4 Prophetic Protocol 45

CHAPTER 5 Use Your Gift! 59

CHAPTER 6 Don't Have a Burger King Mentality! 65

CHAPTER 7 The Timing of Prophetic Words 73

CHAPTER 8 The Prophetic Mindset 79

CHAPTER 9 Prophetic Therapy 83

CHAPTER 10 Prophetic Etiquette 87

PART III The Prophet 91

CHAPTER 11 The Importance of the Prophetic Office 93

CHAPTER 12 A Process Is Attached to Your Calling 97

CHAPTER 13 Encouragement for Misfit Prophets 105

CHAPTER 14 Wrong Prophetic Motives 109

CHAPTER 15 How to Avoid Deception When Prophesying . . 113

CHAPTER 16 Prophets vs. Psychics 117

CHAPTER 17 The Toxic Tongue 123

PART IV The Prophetic Church 127

CHAPTER 18 Not-for-Prophet Churches 129

CHAPTER 19 True Prophetic Houses 137

PART V Resources 143

CHAPTER 20 Confessions, Prayers, and Prophetic Words . . . 145

Foreword

What an exciting time to be alive! God's Word is being declared around the world, and more and more people are moving in prophetic ministry. The subjects of prophets, prophecy, and worship are coming to the forefront of the church. I believe this is a move of the Holy Spirit to release miracles and breakthroughs in the lives of His people.

A growing number of prophetic scribes are also writing on the subject. John Veal is one of those scribes. The subject matter in this book will add to an increasing knowledge of prophets and prophecy. God is stirring His authors to impart knowledge, wisdom, and understanding to the Church. I believe the subject of prophecy needs to be understood if we are to experience the blessings of this amazing manifestation of the Spirit.

John shares from a wealth of experience. He gives his personal testimony and how he developed in prophetic ministry. This book is more than theory and includes relatable experiences to help you understand the process that many prophetic people go through before they fully step out into prophetic ministry. You might identify with some of his experiences in your own life as you read this book.

Churches need to implement proper prophetic protocol when ministering to people. Many today have genuine gifts but lack the proper training to release what God gives them. This book deals with prophetic etiquette, including simple steps that you can learn that will help you make any adjustments in this area. We must operate in excellence if we expect the Word of the Lord to be received.

Prophecy is more than giving someone information. Prophecy can release miracles, healing, and deliverance. Prophecy is supernatural, which is the focus of this book. We are called to live supernatural lifestyles and should expect to receive supernatural breakthroughs as a result of prophecy. We are called to be supernaturally prophetic.

John also challenges the motives of those who minister. Prophetic abuse can occur anytime the prophetic ministry is emphasized. The enemy loves to hurt and damage people through false prophecy and false prophetic ministries. This is why the process of prophetic development is so important.

Many today are being exposed to the prophetic ministry for the first time. We need a foundational knowledge of this as we must base what we do on the Word of God. We also need practical teaching from those with more experience. Samuel helped train the emerging prophets and was a father to them. As a prophetic father, John has a heart to see sons and daughters taught and properly trained to speak as the oracles of God.

He has a love and vision for the church where the role of the prophetic is vital. Prophecy is a key to building strong believers and churches. Pastors would do well to study the subject and teach it to their congregations. Prophets and prophetic ministers need to be connected to the local church. All believers are not prophets, but all can be prophetic.

I pray that as you read this book, God will give you a deeper understanding of this subject. As Proverbs tells us, wisdom is the principal thing. Be blessed as you read and study on the subject of being supernaturally prophetic.

JOHN ECKHARDT
Overseer of Crusaders Church
Author of more than fifty books including *Prophet Arise, Prophetic Activation*, and *God Still Speaks*

Introduction

And Moses said unto him, Enviest thou for my
sake? Would God that all the Lord's people
were prophets, and that the Lord would put
his spirit upon them! (Numbers 11:29)

Supernatural: *departing from what*
is usual or normal especially so as to
appear to transcend the laws of nature.

Welcome! It's no accident that you're reading this book right now. You're here by divine appointment. A supernatural anointing is on this manuscript that I believe will take you to an all-new level in your understanding of prophecy. I wrote this book with the goal of teaching you prophetic principles that will enable you to navigate the realm of the spirit with supernatural precision.

Every born-again believer who is filled with the Holy Ghost can supernaturally prophesy! This book is designated for people with a strong, innate desire to grow prophetically. I believe that my wilderness training, experience, and knowledge in this area will serve you well in developing your own God-given prophetic DNA. As you read this book, you will benefit from my years of success and failure related to the ministry of the prophet. I am truly passionate about training prophets and equipping prophetic people—those individuals who are not necessarily called to be prophets but can operate in the gift of prophecy.

The Lord has graciously opened doors, enabling me to teach all over the world. In my travels, I've been greatly disturbed by the lack of knowledge concerning identity among prophets. Many don't seem to have a revelation of who they are in Him. Fear stands out as one of the biggest obstacles when they attempt to operate in their true prophetic natures. In fact, the enemy uses this as a primary tool to shut the mouths of prophetic people. Satan's done one heck of a job keeping them silent, especially in the church. There are probably few things the devil enjoys more than putting and keeping his hand over the mouths of God's prophets. It's time to take his crusty mitts off your lips and begin to declare what God is saying! It's truly the season to cry loud and spare not (see Isa. 58:1)!

One of my objectives is to demystify the prophetic. Many don't flow in prophecy because they don't fully comprehend it, which breeds fear. My greatest desire is to bring clarity to your calling, understanding to your conditioning (the process), and manifestation of your commissioning. This is one of the most prevalent mandates from the Lord upon my life. When you have a clear view of who you are, you can function in your gift with confidence. I'm not referring to your own natural confidence but to the Lord's supernatural confidence.

My sincere hope is that you'll develop the ability to hear God for yourself. This will benefit you when a prophet is unavailable and you need a word from the Lord. My prayer is that this book will continue to "speak" to you long after I'm gone. I believe this manuscript will shift, train, educate, and reset you.

I'll start by explaining how every born-again, Holy-Ghost-filled believer can prophesy, and then we'll discuss basic prophetic protocols and the office of the prophet. I'll conclude with an informative treatise on what a prophetic people and church should look like. I want to put my years of experience in the palm of your hand or electronic device, at the ready whenever needed. Let's go!

Part I

ALL CAN PROPHESY

CHAPTER 1

My Supernatural Beginnings

And they overcame him by the blood of the Lamb,
and by the word of their testimony; and they loved
not their lives unto the death (Revelation 12:11).

Beverly, your baby will not make it through the night!" Hospital staff made that horrendous declaration to my extremely concerned mother on the day of my birth. During delivery, the umbilical cord became entangled around my neck, very much like a python constricting its prey. As a result, every time my mother pushed and the doctor pulled, I was actually being strangled to death! One of the physicians discovered the problem and mercifully removed the cord from around my neck. When I finally was born, my skin had a bluish hue due to prolonged oxygen deprivation. As a result of the stress placed upon my newborn body, my lungs collapsed. As I lay in the incubator, barely clinging to life, my mother caught the eye of one of the nurses in the operating room, giving her a hopeful look concerning my precarious health. The only response she received was a downward glance and shaking of the head, betraying the death sentence that seemed a foregone conclusion in the natural. Upon hearing the terrible news, my family rallied together in prayer, believing God for a supernatural miracle. My father's mother, my faith-filled grandmother, recited a specific prayer that reverberates in my bones to this day.

"Lord, if you allow him to live, let him be a blessing to his family, friends, and the world."

These words were her petition to the Most High for mercy on my life. The first night of my arrival on earth was wrought with fear, desperation, and hopelessness. The enemy's desire was to take me out, but God had other plans for me. The next day, a miracle occurred that left the entire hospital staff dumbfounded and the doctors amazed! I'd made a complete recovery despite the naysayers and prognosticators that earnestly proclaimed that I wouldn't make it through the night. My family rejoiced and gave all the glory to God.

Ironically, many of those God has ordained as prophets commonly experience this dreadful theme of almost dying at birth. It's as if the enemy of our souls has inside information regarding the divine future of those called by the Lord. He literally seeks to destroy them before they can mature into the mantle that God has placed upon their lives. The coward that he is, Satan relishes attacking us when he feels we're most defenseless. This was the case for me so many years ago.

As a child, I had always felt different, not better than anyone, just different. I would feel utterly alone in a room full of people. Maybe you can relate. Much later, I learned that this was typical of what most people experience when God has a divine plan for them. In my case, I always felt as if someone was with me, guiding me, protecting me, and talking to me. For the record, I'm not crazy! I don't hear voices or see dead people, but I felt a very close and personal relationship with Father God. I instinctively knew that I was special to Him and called to do a work. This feeling was totally internal in nature and value. I couldn't rationalize or quantify it. I just knew it deep in my heart of hearts.

In the subsequent years, I had many dreams about heaven and my assignment. In some of my dreams, I saw myself ministering to many people, speaking the word of the Lord on a platform. During this time, I discovered something about myself. I knew certain things, things I couldn't readily discuss without causing concern to the hearer. At the time, I had no filter. I said exactly what I felt impressed by the Lord to say, no matter what. I told others about their past, present, and future, which frightened them almost as much as it did me. I had no previous experience with this and no one to talk to about my unusual gift. My Aunt Helen called me "the psycho psychic." I wasn't particularly fond of her nickname for me, but I had no idea what I was. Was I really a psychic? Was I a mind reader? I had no clue! Many gifted children also face this same dilemma. They have no idea what or who they are. In fact, their gift is often ridiculed and feared instead of encouraged and cultivated. As a result, I withdrew because I felt as if something was wrong with me. Was this a gift from God or curse of the devil? If this gift was from the Lord, what did God want me to do with it?

I greatly struggled with my identity in Him over the next few years. When I first entered college, I encountered a whole new set of circumstances. I attended North Carolina Central University in Durham, North Carolina, in the Bible Belt. While there, I was challenged by some of the most religious people I'd ever met. They consistently attacked me for almost everything I did: reading *Ebony*, a popular secular magazine; listening to worldly music; wearing certain clothing; going to the movies; dancing; and other imagined offenses. All this and more was sinful behavior in their eyes. All of these warnings about my behavior were followed by, "You're going to hell!"

I was saved at the age of nineteen, not so much out of love, but out of incredible fear of spending an eternity in Hades. I'm just being transparent with you about exactly what I was feeling at the time. The true love for the Lord came much later when I began an authentic relationship with Jesus.

Dead Man Walking

During this time, several incidents happened that significantly changed the entire course of my life. The first occurred as I was walking across my college campus with a friend. The college had numerous small hills that we frequently had to traverse to go back and forth to class. As we were coming down one particular hill, I saw another young man, alone and walking toward us. Our eyes met, and I was almost immediately troubled. From seemingly out of nowhere, I told my friend, "He looks dead."

My buddy replied, laughingly, "Why would you say that?"

"I don't know!" I replied incredulously. Hesitantly, I added, "He just looks dead to me." I now believe that I was seeing into the realm of the supernatural. Through spiritual eyes, the young man had an ashen, grayish tone to his skin. He actually looked like a dead man walking. I don't believe that he heard me, but he gave me a very peculiar look as he passed by. Later that night, to my utter dismay, I heard that this same young man was violently killed! The rumor was that he was repeatedly run over by a car after our school's football game. It was reportedly done maliciously and purposefully due to an altercation at the game.

That evening, disbelief and confusion competed for my attention as I mulled over the events of the day. How did I know that this would happen? In retrospect, I didn't. I had no understanding of what I was seeing until its ultimate manifestation. Lord, I wish I would have known then how to war in the spirit for him; maybe he'd still be alive today. This incident continues to bother me to this day.

Football Hall

The second experience occurred as I was walking in my dorm, thinking about how I was going to live this new life of salvation. I wasn't paying attention to where I was going and ended up venturing into the notorious Football Hall, a corridor that encompassed the entire first floor of my dormitory. It was exclusive to the NCCU football team. Anyone who set foot on that floor was subject to a possible "beat down" by the team. A rumored incident occurred when an unsuspecting freshman made the mistake of walking down Football Hall with two bags full of groceries. Someone suddenly shut off the lights, and when they were turned back on, the hapless freshman lay beaten on the floor next to two torn, empty paper bags. That floor had quite a reputation as you can clearly see.

Now, I found myself in that exact same hall. I kept walking, engaged in thought, mainly concerning the call of God on my life, barely noticing the three burly football players leaning up against the wall. I greeted the group of them, and one of them insincerely responded, "What's up?" He then stated that he hated me, using choice expletives. Another one alerted me to the fact that I was in their space and needed to leave immediately.

I responded, "I'm just walking through." I had no intention of running and surprisingly, very little fear. When God dwells within you, fear no longer plagues you. I truly believe that the closer you become to God, the more alien fear becomes to you. According to First John 4:16-18, God is love, and there is no fear in Him.

I continued my exodus through this labyrinth of hostility only to hear one of them say, "I'll take care of him myself." As I stopped and turned around to face my potential adversary, I saw the largest of the three, who was about 6 feet 6 inches tall, forcefully leap off the wall and proceed menacingly toward me. A sudden boldness arose within me that I now realize was the prompting of the Holy Spirit. I stood my ground, and by the time he reached me, I was prepared for battle, win, lose, or draw. I looked up at him as he stood just inches away from me, so close that I could literally feel his breath. Just as I thought that fighting would be my portion on this particular night, I caught a glimpse of the expression of the young man who towered over me. He was directly in front of me, but he wasn't looking at me; instead, he was staring over and above my shoulder. I have never seen that look on anyone's face before or since! I actually glanced behind me to see if someone else was standing there, but there was no one. I slowly turned and attempted to catch the gaze of the goliath before me. To my amazement, he had already begun turning away.

The hulking young man moved back to the same spot in slow motion, falling against the wall next to his comrades. He stood staring blankly in front of him, absolutely speechless. The silence of Football Hall was deafening that night, at least for me. The regularly rambunctious atmosphere of the hall on the first floor totally changed. In the midst of this supernatural peace, the other two gentlemen with him looked at me in bewilderment. One of them mustered enough energy to nervously say, "You shouldn't be down here!"

I responded with an almost divine calmness, "I'm just walking through." I continued my trek down the hall, wondering what had just happened. Years later, the Lord revealed to me through His Word what my "goliath" saw. He placed the following Scripture in my spirit. *"Are they [angels] not all ministering spirits, sent forth to minister for them who shall be heirs of salvation?"* (Heb. 1:14).

Minister means to serve or wait upon (Strong's #G1247). God has angels that are assigned to us to watch over us in all our ways. I truly believe that the person's intentions to harm me changed when he saw an angel sent by God. I must admit that as this was unfolding, I had no idea that it was the Lord. The following bears repeating. I have never seen this expression on anyone's face before or since. If anyone asked me to recreate it, I couldn't. Based on Scripture, I humbly believe that he saw something greater than me behind me yet over me! This angelic host wouldn't allow any harm to come to me because I was an heir of salvation. I sure would love to ask him what he saw all those years ago, but unfortunately, I never saw him again. If he ever grabs a hold of this book, I pray that the Lord would put it on his heart to reach out to me.

In the years following, I've heard of many similar stories. Many people have been protected by unidentified men or women, unseen by them but visible to their attackers, causing them to flee in terror. Upon learning this, I felt more normal, if that makes sense. I felt as if I wasn't alone in my supernatural experiences. Some of you reading this book can relate because you've had these kinds of encounters and your lives have never been the same since. This is natural in the supernatural lives of prophetic people.

The Voice

The third occurrence that happened around this time was the most amazing of them all. My life—spiritually and naturally— was saved when I was twenty years old and home on summer break from college. It was a very warm night, and I was wearing shorts, a t-shirt, and gym shoes. I was with my good friend, Rob, and we were laughing and talking as we walked along the sidewalk by the main street. Rob pulled out a dark object from his pants as we continued to chat. It was a BB gun, a very realistic-looking facsimile of an actual pistol that shot small pellets instead of bullets. When

I talked to him further, he admitted that the police had detained him on several occasions because of its authentic appearance. We continued our journey into the night and reached a garbage-filled alley. Ignoring the stench and feeling adventurous, we decided to walk through it. We noticed a medium-sized stray dog at the end of the corridor. Demonstrating our immaturity, we decided to shoot the dog with the BB gun. At some point, the gun ended up in my hands. We ran vigorously toward the alarmed canine, which took off, shooting out of the alley like a dart across the main street into another alley. Rob was slightly ahead of me as we followed. As I was sprinting across the street, to my surprise, I heard a voice that seemed to be right at my ear, though no one was visible. The calm yet serious voice warned me, "Take the gun, put it in your shorts, and pull your shirt over it."

I exclaimed in bewilderment to the person that I could not see, "What?" The voice repeated the words, but this time the urgency was laden with authority!

"Take the gun, put it in your shorts, and pull your shirt over it!"

I hollered out loud in total surrender, "Okay!" as I proceeded to do exactly as I was instructed. This whole conversation took place as I was running. A dialogue that should have at least taken a minute ended in mere seconds.

Suddenly, I found myself at the opening of another alley on the right with Rob positioned at my far left. The frightened dog had ventured in seconds before us. We both peered anxiously into the alley, looking for the animal.

As our backs were turned to the street and focused on the dog, two motorcycles pulled up behind us. One of the riders shouted, "Freeze!" As we slowly turned around, we saw two husky bikers, clad in leather vests and blue jeans, with guns drawn! Immediately, we both threw up our hands. The two motorcyclists identified themselves as undercover detectives that were responding to a report of a robbery in that very area. The police officers saw us both running across the street earlier and immediately assumed that we were the culprits. One of them asked what we were doing. I nervously told the detectives that I was home from college on vacation and that we were just chasing a dog. Thankfully, they believed me and didn't frisk either of us. They just warned us to be more careful and rode off into the night.

As we were walking home, it dawned on me. If the BB gun had been in my hand when I turned around to face those under-cover cops, I probably would have been shot! They would've thought that I was carrying a real gun! I don't think that I ever told Rob about it. I'm sure I held back my confession because I didn't want him to think that I was insane. The voice that I heard that night literally saved my life! It didn't say, "I'm the Lord your God," or "This is Michael the archangel," it just simply told me what I needed to know to keep me alive and safe. At the time, I had no idea that God was speaking to me directly or by a divine messenger. How do I know now? I know because of the authority in the voice that I heard. Though I knew it was a male, it seemed like it was both male and female. I know that sounds weird, but it's what I heard at the time. He spoke like a father commanding his son, and I will never forget it as long as I live. This miracle tops all the amazing things that the Lord has done for me and my family.

A short time later, I received the revelation that God had a special call upon my life. I knew then that I was meant to serve Him. The Lord could somehow see my destiny and He cancelled the plan that the devil had for my destruction. He intervened, and my life has never been the same. Glory to God!

These three supernatural experiences confirmed that the Father had called me to do a work for Him. At the time, I had no idea what that was. I didn't find out until many years later. I'd frequently dream about preaching before multitudes of people, but I had dismissed the thought because I had no interest in preaching. During this time, many demonic attacks came against me in an attempt to usurp the call of God on my life. I intend to chronicle these occurrences in another book that will focus on deliverance.

When I returned to NCCU, I immersed myself in Christian culture with my newfound friends. I later made the mistake of sharing my "gift" with them. I couldn't really identify this particular gift, but I knew how to use it. It was raw but very accurate. I began to tell them about specific things related to their pasts. As a result, my "brothers in Christ" became afraid of me and began speaking against me. I was accused of bringing a demonic attack on them. They began calling me "Satan" behind my back! My sense of not belonging, rooted in my childhood, increased to the point where I left NCCU and ended up completing college back in Chicago. I thought, *Is this what I get for sharing my "gift" with my brothers and sisters in Christ?* These people were supposed to love and care about me, yet I received very little encouragement from them. Instead, condemnation and legalism was my portion.

Subsequently, I turned my back on their form of Christianity for the next thirteen years. At the age of thirty-two, I had another supernatural encounter with God that changed the very course of my life to this day. I gave myself fully to the Lord, and He filled me with His precious Holy Spirit. I've been running for the Lord ever since.

The ostracism, ignorance, and fear that I encountered regarding my gift during my college years created a passion in me to stop others who are spiritually gifted from experiencing these same things. I had no mentors to show me how to properly utilize my gift at that time. I couldn't find many books or trainings about it. I didn't know if it was from God or Satan due to the callous words of other Christians who didn't understand the prophetic. To be quite honest with you, for a long time, I had no idea what to call what I was able to do.

Everyone in my immediate family was Catholic. Interestingly enough, most of them could "see." My grandfather, father, and mother all had the same gift that I did. They didn't understand their own gifting, so how could they teach me about mine? As a result, for years, I became quite well acquainted with the isolation that comes with being a prophet. I was educated by the Holy Spirit with very little input from people. I spent time in churches that didn't fully operate or train in the prophetic. This is not an indictment on those ministries. I learned a lot from them, but training in prophetic giftings just wasn't their cup of tea. Years later in my wilderness, I discovered that I was supernaturally prophetic!

CHAPTER 2

What Is Prophecy?

But he that prophesieth speaketh unto
men to edification, and exhortation,
and comfort (1 Corinthians 14:3).

Prophecy is defined as "the foretelling or prediction of what is to come" or "a divinely inspired utterance or declaration."[1] Godly prophecy is an utterance that comes from being filled with the Holy Spirit. In my experience, speaking prophetic words is based upon hearing what the Lord is saying and repeating it. I just listen to God and say what He says. In order to do this, I must *know* His voice. Jesus said in John 10:27, *"My sheep hear my voice, and I know them, and they follow me."* This further confirms that all Holy-Ghost-filled believers can prophesy. If you *know* His voice, you can as well. Does this make you a prophet? No, but we will address that later. The most important factor in the success or failure of prophecy is how well an individual hears God.

Prophecy is comprised of three major components—prophecy (pertaining to the future), words of knowledge (supernatural knowledge about the past), and words of wisdom (divine guidance or advice). These gifts are mentioned in First Corinthians 12. We will go into more detail about this later in this book. A prophet should be able to walk in at least one of these three gifts at all times. Out of the nine gifts of the Spirit, we should desire to prophesy, according to First Corinthians 14:1. Paul instructs us to *"pursue love, yet desire earnestly spiritual gifts, but especially that you may prophesy"* (NASB). This leads me to believe that hearing God and speaking His words is of paramount importance. I can't think of too many other gifts more valuable than being a mouthpiece for God.

Many times, I reluctantly shared my ability to prophesy. I hesitated because of the fearful and confusing reactions from people. In fact, after I was confirmed as a prophet in 2009, my father suggested that I not use the title. He thought that people would think I was nuts. Prophecy during that time was not as popular as it is today when people commonly call themselves prophets of the Most High. Before I walked in the calling of a prophet, I spoke the word of the Lord to people as a pastor. Some of those same people came up to me for ministry, shaking and afraid. I was confused as to why they were so frightened. I learned later that many fear the unknown. When angels appeared to people in the Old Testament, one of the first things that came out their mouths was "Fear not!" When we deal with something unfamiliar, we tend to draw back.

I believe this is what happened to me way back when. Others were fearful because they did not understand this gift. When you're properly educated in the prophetic, feelings of fear slowly subside and confidence replaces fear. The more you know about the prophetic, the more comfortable you will be with prophecy.

At times, I have released a prophetic word that the person did not heed. This sometimes resulted in dire consequences for them. In 2004, on a seemingly normal Sunday, I felt a strong urge to give a prophetic word to a young man who was a member of our church. I told him to stay away from guns and watch his so-called friends. He walked away, perplexed, stating that he didn't own a gun and didn't hang with anyone dangerous. He subsequently left our ministry. Six or seven years later, I received a letter from him, stating: "I believe that you are a true prophet of God. You gave me a word about watching my friends and staying away from guns. It didn't make sense to me then because I rarely hung with anyone and didn't own a gun, but it does now. A so-called friend asked me to come over. While on my way, three guys jumped out and attempted to rob me. I was set up. I pulled out my gun and shot all three dead. I'm currently in prison for forty-plus years. Believe it or not, I have peace."

After this and many similar situations, I've learned to trust what I'm hearing from the Lord when it comes to prophecy, and so should you. Stick with what God says, and you can't go wrong concerning the operation of your gift. Don't be swayed by the wisdom of man. I've spoken words of prophecy that caused some to become very upset with me because it wasn't what they wanted to hear. However, some came back later and apologized after slandering my name, admitting that I was right. I have no fear of saying what

God tells me. Some might not agree, but I will not compromise the prophetic words received from Father God, and neither should you!

Note

1.   Dictionary.com, Dictionary.com Unabridged, s.v. "prophecy," Random House, Inc., http://www.dictionary.com/browse/prophecy.

CHAPTER 3

You Are Inherently Prophetic!

Pursue love, yet desire earnestly spiritual
gifts, but especially that you may prophesy
(1 Corinthians 14:1 NASB).

Whether you know it or not, as a Spirit-filled believer, you are inherently prophetic. *Inherent* is defined as belonging to the basic nature of someone or something. In essence, your gift was given to you by God to bless others. The gift of prophecy is quite literally embedded within your genes on a deep spiritual level. It belongs to you and resides in you and should flow from you organically and supernaturally. When you walk in continued ignorance of the gift at your disposal, stagnation and alienation of your God-given prophetic process occurs. Prophetically speaking on the Lord's behalf is not only germane to the prophet, but it is a divine right given by God to every believer (Strong's #G4394).

I used to believe that only prophets could prophesy. However, I was completely wrong. In First Samuel 10, we have biblical insight regarding something incredibly prophetic happening to a person that was not necessarily a prophet. Saul, the son of Kish, had just been anointed as king over all of Israel and almost immediately received a word through the prophet Samuel. In First Samuel 9:20, we find Saul overly concerned with locating his donkeys, which had been missing for three days. Samuel the seer instructed him not to worry about them because they had already been found. It never ceases to amaze me that, when God has a supernatural destiny in store for you, the devil will attempt to keep you focused on your spiritual asses! I'm referring to *donkeys in the spirit* that are stubborn, refusing to move out of your way in relation to the call of God upon your life. Once you've identified them, you gain the ability to defeat them. Knowledge of them equates to power over them. These spiritual asses have already been discovered, but the devil will convince you that they're still lost. This is essentially a demonic smokescreen to cause you to doubt your true identity (in Saul's case, becoming king) and focus on a false one (finding donkeys).

In Matthew 4, the Holy Spirit led Jesus into the wilderness to be tempted of the devil. One of the first things that Satan did was attempt to remove the focus of our Lord off the supernatural (God's will) and on the natural (man's needs). Starting at verse 3, Lucifer began his temptation of Christ with, *"If thou be the Son of*

God, command these stones to be turned into bread." This appealed to immediate human needs, not godly directives. Satan used "if thous" several times in this chapter alone. Jesus always answered him with the Word of God, and so should you! Whenever he comes saying, "If you were a prophet..." hit him over the head with the Word. I believe the enemy does this to intentionally remove your focus off the Lord's will and onto your own will.

Saul was about to rule a kingdom and have a tremendous experience in the supernatural of the Most High, and all he could think about was finding lost asses! Sometimes, we become so entangled in the affairs of men that we lose sight of our heavenly assignment.

During this time, Saul was humbled by the attention from the prophet, as evidenced in First Samuel 9:21. *"And Saul said, Am not I a Benjamite, of the smallest of the tribes of Israel? and my family the least of all the families of Benjamin? wherefore then thou speakest so to me?"*

God promotes the humble! *Humility precedes ordained, prophetic encounters.* According to Numbers 12:3, Moses was the meekest man on the face of the earth. He was also the most mightily used person of God at that time. We must conclude that meekness is might in the eyes of the Lord. *Meek* is defined as submissive, gentle, obedient, unassuming, and humble. Yes, Moses had all these attributes. In addition, he was also a prophet. Arrogance can never be and should never be attributed to the oracles of the Most High. When a so-called seer of God walks in pride, run! Pride didn't get a hold of King Saul until much later, but that's another story. In First Samuel 10:1, Samuel anointed Saul with oil, poured it upon his head, and kissed him, saying, *"Is it not because the Lord hath anointed thee to be captain [prince] over His inheritance [His heritage Israel]?"* Afterward, Samuel released three prophesies over Saul. The first dealt with finding the lost donkeys. The second one was about getting two loaves of bread. The third one spoke of coming to the hill of God and meeting a company of prophets. I believe that the "hill of God" mentioned in verse 5 relates to elevation in Him.

> *After that thou shalt come to the hill of God, where is the garrison of the Philistines: and it shall come to pass, when thou art come thither to the city, that thou shalt meet a company of prophets coming down from the high place with a psaltery, and a tabret, and a pipe, and a harp, before them; and they shall prophesy: And the Spirit of the Lord will come upon thee, and thou shalt prophesy with them, and shalt be turned into another man* (1 Samuel 10:5-6).

Saul had to head up higher to allow prophecy to come down! Notice that as he went up, he met a company of prophets coming down from not just from *a* high place, but from *the* high place. Just any old high place will not do; you must seek the specific high place where you are called.

In seeking prophetic encounters, you must allow God to direct your eyes to look higher, not lower. When you allow your vision to see as God sees, like Saul, you will see a company of prophets coming toward you with musical instruments, prophesying! According to First Samuel 10:6, the Spirit of the Lord was going to come on Saul mightily, and he would be a prophet with them, turning him into another man. All these things came to pass later in the chapter, but I want to bring something else to your attention.

When Saul was around the prophets, he became prophetic. First Samuel 10:10 states that *"the Spirit of the Lord came upon him mightily"* (NASB) so that he spoke under divine inspiration while he was with them. Saul had never done this before. There is no biblical evidence that Saul was enrolled in Samuel's school of the prophets. He didn't have a degree from "Sam's Prophetic University" or "Samuel's School for the Gifted." According to verse 11, he spoke by inspiration while among the "schooled" prophets. The question arose, asking if Saul was actually a prophet. My answer to this question is no, because verse 13 of that same chapter states that Saul's inspired speaking ended. I think that it ended because he left the company of seers. When he was around the prophets, what was in them activated what was in him! I am referring to the prophetic DNA or gift that resided in him. Saul's divine constitution allowed him to prophesy with apparently seasoned prophets for a specific period of time.

This still happens to Spirit-filled believers today. If you are around prophets or prophetic people long enough, prophecy will rub off on you! If you're too close to it, you will catch it. I have found that prophecy is contagious and easily passed to others. Everyone has a spot inside them just waiting for the prophetic to completely fill it. A seer seed in all of us germinates once watered by prophetic activity. In order to move your prophetic genes, they need to be activated and exercised. You can do this through *prophetic activation*, which is simply a stirring up of the gift that already dwells within you. I liken it to strengthening the human muscles through resistance training. The more resistance placed upon a specific muscle area over time, the stronger and more developed it becomes. Your gift of prophecy will respond in the same manner. The more you exercise it, the stronger it becomes. Activations are paramount to this process. Not only do they increase the capacity of your gift, but they also help increase the intensity of your gift. Activations assist in not having to rely on someone else to hear God for you. It augments your innate ability to hear Him for yourself. These activations can cause your spiritual ears to tune into the Lord's frequency and access your inherently prophetic nature.

I've seen many people who were not necessarily prophetic but who became prophetic through activation exercises. Not only does an activation ignite the prophetic gift in them, but the subsequent shaking causes other gifts around it to be stirred up as well. After one such activation, one woman told me that her hands felt hot. I discerned that this was a sign of the gift of healing and told her so. Later, she began operating in the gift of healing. This type of thing has happened in nearly every activation that I've ever done. Many wonderful testimonies of prophetic awakenings have resulted from these prophetic activations. For further information on how I can help activate you or your church or ministry, please contact me at supernaturallyprophetic@gmail.com.

During one of these activation sessions, I had a revelation. As I laid hands on a woman to activate her prophetic gift, I saw three gifts inside of her, each varied in size. They actually looked like gift-wrapped presents, bows and all. One gift was bigger than all the others, which seemed to be her dominant gift. I believe that everyone has a few gifts, but usually one is primary or bigger than the others. For example, I discerned a prophetic gift as the largest of her gifts. The other gifts, such as healing, faith, and discernment were relatively small, often due to infrequent or even no use. Again, this is very similar to the human muscle. Through consistent, prolonged neglect, muscle atrophies or shrinks. The smaller it gets from a lack of activity, the weaker the muscle becomes. Your God-given gifts operate in much the same manner. The less you use them, the smaller or weaker they become. The gifts the Lord gives you never go away, according to Romans 11:29. *"For the gifts and calling of God are without repentance."*

The Lord will not give you something and then demand it back. However, gifts might decrease in strength if they are not used. Anything you don't exercise weakens over time. I'm definitely stronger prophetically than I was the day I entered ministry.

In 2002, God instructed me to use my gift, and I obeyed. I haven't stopped using it since. The more I participated in the process of providing prophetic ministry to others, the more proficient I became. Sadly, many in the Body of Christ have a multitude of untapped gifts. These God-given gifts are wrapped but never opened or used. This is a travesty because a lot of people need what the Lord has bestowed within you. We must come to the realization that gifts are truly meant to be given. Your heaven-sent abilities are the key to someone's breakthrough. Many are impatiently waiting for them to manifest in you. You are called to minister to certain people in the world. You might not be called to everyone, but you are called to someone.

Over the years, my gift became bigger, stronger, and more precise as I exercised it. My advice to emerging prophets and prophetic people is to use your prophetic gift as much as possible. The more you use it, the more robust it becomes. Think about it. The longer that you do anything, the better you become at it. Recently, I ministered at a prophetic conference in Sheboygan, Wisconsin. I prophesied to more than two hundred people over a three-day period. I did this non-stop for almost three hours each day, twice a day without any breaks. On the final day, my voice was just about gone, and I was exhausted, but I must admit, my prophetic gift went to another level.

When your gift is stretched, it strengthens! When it's pushed or pulled upon regularly, it increases in depth. The weight of your gift becomes heavier, and is now characterized by fatness from being consistently fed over time. *"And it shall come to pass in that day, that his burden shall be taken away from off thy shoulder, and his yoke from off thy neck, and the yoke shall be destroyed because of the anointing"* (Isa. 10:27). The context of this verse includes the ox becoming so fat (anointed) that the yoke breaks.

Similar to "eating" the Word of God, you feed your gift every time you use it. When you routinely neglect daily Scripture reading, you might find yourself becoming spiritually weak. In Matthew 4:4, Jesus told the devil that *"man shall not live by bread alone, but by every word that proceedeth out of the mouth of God."* The Bible is the living Word of God, and you need to eat of it daily in order to provide sustenance, making you fatter in the spirit. Fatness equates to weightiness, which is a positive thing spiritually. Likewise, if you go a week without food, you will feel worn out, depleted, and lethargic. You must be nourished both physically and spiritually in order to maintain a synergistic level between the spiritual and natural aspects of your prophetic gift.

My spiritual mother, Ruth Brown, used to demand that I speak prophetically concerning various issues in her life. She wrote *Destroying the Works of Witchcraft Through Fasting and Prayer,* which I enthusiastically recommend that you add to your literary library. Her orders used to greatly annoy me, and I didn't hesitate to let her know. In response to my rebellion, she rebuked me sharply and stated firmly yet lovingly that this would increase my accuracy. Mother Brown added that each time she challenged me in this way, I was always correct. In retrospect, she was right. As much as I disliked her methods, mother knew best. Today, I use similar methods to challenge emerging prophets whom I mentor or activate. They don't really like it either, but the benefits they experience in increasing their prophetic exactness tend to outweigh their reservations.

I've gained much of what I've learned about the prophetic from God in the isolation of the wilderness. When I was learning how to walk in the prophetic, I did not know of books to read or of schools to attend. I was very similar to the biblical prophet, Amos, who honestly responded to Amaziah, the priest who falsely accused him of conspiracy against Jeroboam, king of Israel.

Then Amaziah the priest of Bethel sent to Jeroboam king of Israel, saying, Amos hath conspired against thee in the midst of the house of Israel: the land is not able to bear all his words. For thus Amos saith, Jeroboam shall die by the sword, and Israel shall surely be led away captive out of their own land. Also Amaziah said unto Amos, O thou seer, go, flee thee away into the land of Judah, and there eat bread, and prophesy there: But prophesy not again any more at Bethel: for it is the king's chapel, and it is the king's court. Then answered Amos, and said to Amaziah, I was no prophet, neither was I a prophet's son; but I was an herdman, and a gatherer of sycomore fruit: And the Lord took me as I followed the flock, and the Lord said unto me, Go, prophesy unto my people Israel (Amos 7:10-15).

Here, Amos' response to Amaziah's accusation was that he was not a prophet or a son of a prophet, a schooled seer. In the Old Testament, the students within a school of the prophets were referred to as the sons of the prophets. Amos had never received formal prophetic training. He was a student of no one in reference to prophecy. Everything that he knew of the prophetic was birthed in the wilderness apart from formal education. This environment is truly the "school of hard knocks."

However, a lack of training does not negate the raw power within a prophet. Sometimes, an Amos will be equipped with a Samuel anointing. What I mean by that is that some prophets will have little if any formal education from man but instead will only have instruction directly from God. As such, they will be able to give prophetic words that are very similar to those from "schooled" prophets. This training, like what Jesus endured during His temptation in utter isolation, uses the wilderness as a classroom.

In retrospect, I didn't think that I was a prophet and had no desire to be one. However, as Amos 7:17 states, God took me from my current course in life and told me to prophesy to His people. I believe that He will do the same with some of you reading this book. The Lord wants you to identify the supernatural prophetic gift that has resided in you since birth.

My strong conviction is that you can inherit the gift of prophecy. Prophetic abilities can be found in family lines. My father, mother, and grandfather were extremely gifted in forthtelling or foretelling (prophecy). They could all accurately tell me things that they had no earthly way of knowing. These same gifts seem to have been summarily passed down to me. I relate this to an actual inheritance, when a parcel of land, property, or money is handed down from generation to generation. Many in the Body of Christ have inherited these gifts but have no clue how to use them. For example, someone might give you a brand-new vehicle, but you might not know how to drive. One of several things will likely happen.

1. The car will sit in your driveway, slowly rusting from neglect.

2. You will try to drive it, hitting just about everything in sight, severely damaging your gift.

3. You will first learn how to drive by following instructions and practicing so that you can fully enjoy your new car.

Your prophetic gift functions in much the same manner. You must be trained to properly operate in it before you can effectively use it. Sure, you might have a natural inclination to use a supernatural asset, but you won't enjoy the full use of your abilities without continuing to educate yourself in its intricacies. For this reason, we have been assaulted by unbalanced and untrained prophetic words.

This occurs when so-called prophets release false words in the Name of the Lord. They're usually uncaring in regard to accuracy but are only concerned with keeping up with the Joneses. They're just trying to do what seems popular at the moment.

This is very similar to the vagabond Jews who fancied themselves exorcists in Acts 19. They tried to cast out devils from a man by using the Name of Jesus whom Paul preached. They had no relationship with Jesus yet wanted to operate in the "gift" of deliverance. On this particular occasion, those seven sons of Sceva were met with a demon that challenged them. *"Jesus, I know, and Paul I know: but who are ye?"* Subsequently, the demon-possessed man leapt upon the sons, beating them. He left them naked and wounded so that they fled from the house. They failed in delivering this individual due to their lack of a personal relationship and knowledge of Jesus Christ.

This is what happens when some attempt to prophesy without knowing the intimate dynamics of prophecy. They end up being beaten down and hurt by the enemy through the criticisms, doubt, and condemnation of others. This might cause them to run from their gift rather than embrace it. Like Jonah, they literally and figuratively become prophets on the run. This is becoming more and more common. Satan desires to keep you ignorant of your identity as a new creation by limiting your access to knowledge through offense. The spirit of offense has derailed many a gifted seer. This conniving demon wants to hinder people by clouding their vision with perceived and real emotional attacks. This spirit can cause people to allow their flesh to overshadow the directions from the Lord concerning the operation of their gift. When it comes to the prophetic, they refuse to take the time to "read" the instructions from the Lord! They are not willing to pay the price for the manual or the mantle (the office).

I don't believe that those who are inaccurate are all false, but I do think that most are presumptuous. *Presumptuous* means over-stepping proper bounds or taking liberties. This transpires in many prophetic ministries around the world when people assume what God says instead of waiting to hear what He's really saying.

> *When a prophet speaketh in the name of the Lord, if the thing follow not, nor come to pass, that is the thing which the Lord hath not spoken, but the prophet hath spoken it presumptuously: thou shalt not be afraid of him* (Deuteronomy 18:22).

The Scripture above essentially says that if a prophet speaks a word that the Lord did not say, he or she spoke it presumptuously, meaning that it was given without permission or unwarranted. When a prophet gives a word without God's permission, they are not necessarily a false prophet, but they are inaccurate concerning that particular prophecy. Notice in this passage that the prophet is not referred to as a false prophet but as a prophet toward the end of this verse. When a seer gives a prophecy that doesn't come to pass, he or she is not a false prophet but just presumptuous. I've witnessed seasoned prophets give an inaccurate word, possibly due to simply missing the word of the Lord or adding to what He's said to them. The person might be tired, preoccupied, or fighting something physical or emotional. I strongly encourage prophetic people to stop prophesying when extremely tired as exhaustion can cause them to draw more from the flesh than the spirit. When I experience any type of immense fatigue, I make it a habit to stop. While the supernatural grace of God can stave off exhaustion at times, I recommend that you cease your utterances if that's not occurring. This will greatly improve your chances of not missing what the Lord is saying at that particular moment.

At the end of Deuteronomy 18:22, we are instructed not to be afraid of this prophet. Why? Probably because he's a novice in dire need of enrollment in a solid school of the prophets. Presumptuous prophets actually hear a word from the Lord and then make the crucial error of adding in things that God didn't say. For example, God gives you the word *lasagna* and nothing else while prophesying to an individual. You decide to add garlic bread, salad, and soda pop to the prophetic word. The Lord never said these three things, but you did. The prophecy is mostly inaccurate because of the series of false words that followed the initial true one. These extra words originated from you, not from God. People commonly make this mistake and habitually declare what the Lord didn't tell them to decree. The best way to be and to remain accurate is to only say what the Lord is saying. Don't add your opinions or feelings to the words He's given you. If you closely follow this practice of hearing His voice and speaking only His word, you will be supernaturally prophetic.

Many erroneously assume today that they've spoken on behalf of the Lord. This occurs because they have not allowed adequate time for their gifts to be sharpened by prophets more seasoned than they. Every prophet should have a mentor, an experienced and trusted advisor. The mentor that you choose should not be at the same spiritual level that you are. In fact, a wise practice is to align with mentors who are at least several levels above you in experience, wisdom, and knowledge. Otherwise, you will fall into the trap of "the blind leading the blind."

The Old Testament illustrates this principle. In those days, prophets were trained by seasoned prophets, not kings. They needed to be instructed and mantled by someone who walked in the same gifting. For example, Elijah mentored Elisha. In general, the strongest prophets first learn to walk in their gifting by sitting at the feet of and by serving other prophets. These fathers have the spiritual DNA or makeup to conceive and birth people of prophecy. This training is similar to the germination process of a seed. Through watering, light, soil, and time, that seed will grow into what it was pre-programmed to be and will reproduce after its own kind. Prophetic seeds produce prophetic offspring.

> *And God said, Let the earth bring forth grass, the herb yielding seed, and the fruit tree yielding fruit after his kind, whose seed is in itself, upon the earth: and it was so. And the earth brought forth grass, and herb yielding seed after his kind, and the tree yielding fruit, whose seed was in itself, after his kind: and God saw that it was good. And the evening and the morning were the third day (Genesis 1:11-13).*

As with all men, the seed is in the prophet. The prophet inseminates the sons/daughters with divinely directional prophetic words in order for them to produce prophetically, which simply means that mature or senior prophets are the most appropriate people to prepare and mantle other prophets. They have a distinct DNA within them that corresponds and spiritually speaks to the genetic make-up of emerging prophets. As Saul met the prophets coming down a hill and was activated, so will you be activated if you surround yourself with true prophetic companies. The longer you're around gatherings that include strong seers, the more likely that inherent gifts of prophecy will manifest. The prophetic has an intrinsic propensity to be contagious and to easily spread. A spiritually genetic design lies within every believer that includes a prophetic gene. This spiritual DNA activates in the midst of an atmosphere that is conducive to prophecy. As an inherently prophetic person, you need to stay by the fire of foretelling. If you remain close to the flames long enough, you'll become warm and will soon operate in the prophetic supernaturally!

Part II

PROPHECY 101

CHAPTER 4

Prophetic Protocol

For ye may all prophesy one by one, that all may learn, and all may be comforted. And the spirits of the prophets are subject to the prophets. For God is not the author of confusion, but of peace, as in all churches of the saints (1 Corinthians 14:31-33).

When I visit prophetic ministries, I look for certain things that relate to prophetic protocol. If I see that these protocols are absent, I'm immediately concerned. I have seen so much tomfoolery in relation to teaching and training within the Body of Christ that I have grown a bit jaded when it comes to advertised "authentic" ministry regarding prophecy. We have many self-proclaimed social media prophets who are untrained and untested, giving inaccurate words of prophecy to the masses. This can cause a phony perception of all things prophetic. Some might be dissuaded from embarking on their own prophetic journey due to frequent false words that are supposedly from the Lord.

I've witnessed a husband receive a word from a prophet that his wife would have a baby. The prophet confidently announced to them that they would be pregnant that year. They had been struggling to conceive for a relatively long time but to no avail. However, it never happened—not that year, nor the ones that followed. As a result, after that, the husband totally shunned anyone who attempted to prophesy to him. If a prophet came to his church, he made sure that he was ill on that particular day. I think that a lot of people feel this way. A multitude of prophets claim that what they say is of God, but their words do not come to pass.

Sometimes the fault is not in the gift but in the absence of the knowledge of basic fundamentals of prophetic ministry. I've written this section to address tenets that every prophet or prophetic person should know before ministering. This section will help demystify aspects of foundational prophetic ministry. The mistakes in the delivery of prophecy have been disheartening, and this lack of knowledge concerning the prophetic has sadly destroyed many a life.

> *My people are destroyed for lack of knowledge: because thou hast rejected knowledge, I will also reject thee, that thou shalt be no priest to me: seeing thou hast forgotten the law of thy God, I will also forget thy children* (Hosea 4:6).

This occurs primarily due to untrained and underdeveloped prophets whose zeal far outweighs their conditioning, specifically their training, experience, and education in all things prophetic. Far too often, we have emerging prophets operating in arenas that are way beyond their levels of clearance. They desire to operate as generals when they're only corporals, which usually stems from a lack of patience. A process is always married to the calling. This process or conditioning has to happen prior to the commissioning by God.

Some prematurely venture out into water when they're not prepared to swim. They lack the knowledge concerning how to stay afloat in these unchartered waters and thus find themselves in dire straits. When other, more seasoned prophets already used to treading water venture out to help, the novice prophet refuses assistance, thinking that they don't need help. The senior prophet ends up in trouble as well because of the panic and flailing of the drowning prophetic beginner. The senior prophet is then forced to cease their life-saving efforts and leave the emerging prophet where he or she is.

Another common saying applies here. "You can lead a horse to water, but you can't make him drink." If emerging seers refuse direction from older, wiser, and more experienced ones, this will result in unbalanced teaching. The blind should not be leading the blind.

Prophesying with an Unholy Spirit

There are people who have the ability to prophesy without the indwelling of the Holy Ghost. Some prophets in the Old

Testament had an "unholy spirit" that provided them with the means to give words of prophecy. An unholy spirit is simply a spirit that's not holy or sent by the Most High. It is a demonic spirit that inspires prophetic people to say things that God didn't say. Not every prophet mentioned in the Bible was a prophet of God, such as the prophets of Baal, Ashtoreth, etc. These prophets (false because they did not belong to the Lord) actually spent their lives mimicking the true prophets of God who declared the unadulterated word of Jehovah! Satan is a brazen counterfeiter of all that is holy. His goal is to pervert the holy, making it unholy. Demonically inspired prophetic deliveries are temporal in nature and doubtful in outcome. They don't last and might not come to pass. They are fraught with conditions that are intended to keep you bound to men and not God. Satan literally "gifts" you to get you. He has an almost uncontrollable tendency to "bless" you to keep you. The woman with the spirit of divination in the following passage is a prime example of a person guided to speak prophetically by an unholy spirit.

> *And it came to pass, as we went to prayer, a certain damsel possessed with a spirit of divination met us, which brought her masters much gain by soothsaying: The same followed Paul and us, and cried, saying, These men are the servants of the most high God, which shew unto us the way of salvation. And this did she many days. But Paul, being grieved, turned and said to the spirit, I command thee in the name of Jesus Christ to come out of her. And he came out the same hour. And when her masters saw that the hope of their gains was gone, they caught Paul and Silas, and*

drew them into the marketplace unto the rulers (Acts 16:16-19).

Surprisingly, what the woman with the spirit of divination stated was accurate. Paul and Silas *were* the servants of the Most High God who showed us the way of salvation. Paul's discernment let him know that she was operating by a false spirit. He commanded the spirit of divination to leave her in Jesus' Name, and it did. She was no longer able to soothsay. According to the *King James Dictionary*, a soothsayer is one who foretells future events without inspiration. In other words, this woman prophesied without any type of divine inspiration. As a result of Paul's on-the-spot deliverance session, the damsel could no longer make money for her masters.

From this, we can learn that Satan's "gifts" don't last and are subject to the power of God. Since the beginning of time, the wicked one has always used the truth to establish his lies. He did so when he tricked Eve in Genesis 3 into eating forbidden fruit. He twisted Scripture when he tried to tempt Jesus in Matthew 4. In both cases, the devil used God's words, His truth, and then added his lies. Please remember that Satan's prophets will intentionally get some things right and some things wrong. They seek to deceive to bring you to a conclusion void of any guidance from the Lord.

Today, other prophets might operate in unholy behavior, but even so, their prophetic gift comes from God. God's nature is not to take back what He's already given people. A prophetic gift from the Lord is irrevocable. Once the Lord has bestowed a gift upon a person, they have it for life. Prophecies that originate with God are utterances that are attached to being filled with the Holy Spirit. In fact, prophecy is one of the nine gifts of the Spirit mentioned in the Scriptures below.

> *Now there are diversities of gifts, but the same Spirit. And there are differences of administrations, but the same Lord. And there are diversities of operations, but it is the same God which worketh all in all. But the manifestation of the Spirit is given to every man to profit withal. For to one is given by the Spirit the word of wisdom; to another the word of knowledge by the same Spirit; To another faith by the same Spirit; to another the gifts of healing by the same Spirit; To another the working of miracles; to another prophecy; to another discerning of spirits; to another divers kinds of tongues; to another the interpretation of tongues: But all these worketh that one and the selfsame Spirit, dividing to every man severally as he will* (1 Corinthians 12:4-11).

Remember, a word of wisdom (divine advice or direction) and a word of knowledge (divine knowledge of the past) are both components of the prophetic. Words of wisdom, knowledge, and prophecy are used interchangeably or in unison when ministering prophetically. A competent prophet will often flow seamlessly between all three gifts when ministering. All the gifts from God are designed to point others toward Jesus Christ, not ourselves.

Prophetic Politeness

The absence of prophetic politeness in some of today's so-called prophetic churches is alarming. Prophetic politeness means the proper etiquette in prophetic relationships or encounters. Beyond a lack of common courtesy, I've also witnessed this blatant spiritual rudeness on various social media platforms, which is becoming bolder. At times, people will come up to me without a "hello" or formal introduction and ask me for a prophetic word. This happens to me electronically through emails, texts, and on social media. It is both wrong and in poor taste to say to or inbox a prophet with any salutation beginning with phrases, such as, "Where my word at?" or "You got a word for me?" or "I hear you a prophet, what's up?" Please note that the use of Ebonics here was intentional for effect and emphasis. My point is that these people did not greet me first. Instead, they just "barged in," demanding that the prophet instantly produce a word. This is wrong on so many levels although I've learned to chalk up such behavior to ignorance.

I'd rather choose to believe that people are not consciously being crass but that they are just hungry. They're hungry for true words from authentic oracles of God, not pretenders. Many have encountered charlatans and experienced a literal famine in regard to hearing words that bear witness with their spirits. We should always be mindful that prophets of the Most High are not psychics and shouldn't be treated as such. I've learned to ignore such seemingly selfish behavior. I no longer feel bad about not caving in to the deluge of requests for a word from strangers. Believe me, I used to, but God freed me from such condemnation.

If you desire a word from the Lord from a prophet, you can follow this basic protocol. Begin your inquiry with, "Hello, how are you?" and tell the person a little bit about yourself. You'll probably receive a better response along with the answer from

God that you're looking for. I've seen a trend of people totally depending on the prophet rather than taking the time to hear from God for themselves. God still speaks to individuals. This is one of the reasons that I train prophetic people to hear from God for themselves rather than relying on the next prophet to come to town. You know what I'm talking about—the one who charges you $800 to give you a word from the Lord. John 10:4-5 tells us that the sheep follow Him for they know His voice. We cannot carry out the Lord's instructions without being familiar with His voice, for the foundation of prophetic utterances is *knowing God's voice.* Once you know His voice, you cut out the middle man and put yourself in a position to receive prophetic words without the filters of flesh! Prophecy is listening to God and simply repeating what He says, which will help you to be 100 percent accurate unless you miss God or misidentify the voice that's speaking to you as yourself or the enemy instead of God. These three voices (God, Satan, and yourself) constantly contend for your attention. You must be able to distinguish between each one, which is done through discernment and familiarity.

We should use our supernatural senses to identify which one of the three is speaking to us. We must become familiar with each voice. This can be done through consistent and active listening, especially during our times of prayer. When I do prophetic training, I encourage emerging prophets and prophetic people to *know* who's talking to them. You do this by not just praying but by listening so that you will *know* His voice. Listen more than you speak at these times. Each of these three has a distinct cadence that you will become accustomed to.

The Lord Touches the Mouths of His Prophets

Scripture lets us know that He will touch the mouths of prophets and pour in His words as He did with Jeremiah. God did this throughout the Old Testament. If you were a prophet of the Lord back then, your lips were touched by the master. With the touch come the words. The tactile and the sound have a symbiotic relationship where one cannot function properly without the other. God's touch is pregnant with prophecy. When He touches your mouth, your orifice begins to fill with His words. With this filling comes release. Whenever you are full of anything, you must expel it. The Lord expects you to pour out the sayings with which He's filled you. That's why some prophets feel as if they're pregnant with prophecy and as if the words are ready to burst forth. *"Then the Lord put forth his hand, and touched my mouth. And the Lord said unto me, Behold, I have put my words in thy mouth"* (Jer. 1:9).

Like He did with the prophet Jeremiah, God still touches the mouths of His prophets today. All you have to do is to allow the words He gives you to be released and loosed by simply opening your mouth and saying them. It really is that simple. Remember, any Holy-Ghost-filled believer can prophesy. If that's you, *prophesy*. Say what He's telling you to say. If you can hear His voice, you can say what He's said.

Prophetic Dos and Don'ts

The Dos

How to Receive a Word

1. Do listen to every word when you're receiving a prophecy. Too many speak in tongues during this time when they should be listening. You might want to record the word on your electronic device or have someone else record it for you.

2. Do your research on the prophet before you allow him or her to minister to you. Look them up on the Internet.

How to Give a Word

1. Do encourage—edify, exhort, and comfort—others through prophetic words.

2. Do ask before giving a prophetic word to someone.

3. Do seek prophetic training if you're a prophet before walking in the office of a prophet.

4. Do allow a senior prophet to mentor you. Make sure that your mentor is at least two or three levels above you in wisdom, experience, and knowledge.

5. Do press in to what the Lord is saying.

6. Do speak the truth in love. Prophecy is grounded in love.

7. Do exactly what the Holy Spirit instructs you to do.

8. Do use prophecy to guide others concerning the Lord's will.

9. Do allow prophecy to point others to Jesus Christ, not yourself.

10. Do prophesy with humility yet with boldness and authority.

11. Do pray before you speak.

12. Do speak a word in season.

13. Do admonish through prophetic words.

14. Do maintain a prophetic mindset or mentality.

The Don'ts

Don'ts When Receiving a Word

1. Don't allow a prophet to minister to your spouse unless you are present if possible.

Don'ts When Giving a Word

1. Don't exchange money for prophecy. Remember Simon the sorcerer in Scripture. I will elaborate on this further in Chapter 16.

2. Don't lay hands on anyone without asking permission first, or you might get hit.

3. Don't lay hands on or prophesy to a wife without first asking the husband. The husband is the head.

4. Don't say "thus saith the Lord" before or after giving a prophetic word if you're unsure that God said it. This phrase was used in biblical times for prophets to identify whose god they were speaking on behalf of. All prophets are not from the God of Abraham, Isaac, and Jacob.

5. Don't always prophesy doom and gloom. If you tend toward these types of prophecies, you might be dealing with a spirit of rejection as a root cause.

6. Don't prophesy to people you don't like unless God instructs you to.

7. Don't spend a lot of time in dialogue before and during prophetic ministry.

8. Don't ask questions of those you are prophesying to because you might allow the answers to guide your prophetic flow instead of letting God guide you.

9. Don't compete prophetically.

10. Don't give prophetic words based on appearance.

11. Don't tell everyone that they're apostles.

12. Don't ever use prophecy to control others.

13. Don't be lifted up in pride regarding your prophetic gift. Always bring attention to the Giver, not the gift. It will keep you humble.

14. Don't be afraid or intimidated when releasing the word of the Lord.

15. Don't allow others to prostitute your gift.

16. Don't prophesy when you're extremely tired as you might have a tendency to speak carnally when you are exhausted.

17. Don't give words about marriage, pregnancy, moving, and extremely personal information unless you are confident that the Lord released you to do so.

CHAPTER 5

Use Your Gift!

As every man hath received the gift, even so
minister the same one to another, as good stewards
of the manifold grace of God (1 Peter 4:10).

When I minister, I make it a habit to try to pray or prophesy over everyone in the house. Can I get a witness? I do this because I may never have an opportunity to speak to those particular individuals again. The idea is to maximize my supernatural, God-given abilities for the benefit of as many recipients as possible. An underused gift has a tendency to become stagnant and difficult to use over time. For example, if you receive an airplane as a gift and let it sit in the hangar for an extended period of time, it will lose the ability to fly. The mechanisms that enable flight will need a total overhaul due to idleness. The same can happen with an idle gift. Allow me to be clear here. I'm not saying that you will lose your gift, but I am saying that it can collect dust. Scripture lets us know that the gifts and calling of God are without repentance, which means that He'll never take them back.

> For the gifts and calling of God are without repentance (Romans 11:29).

The infrequent use of your gifts will cause them to stay wrapped without ever being fully opened. Once you've identified your gift, use it to the fullest. I am bothered when prophets prophesy to three or four people in a meeting when hundreds desire a word. I sometimes see prophets who are so gifted that they can call out names, phone numbers, bank account numbers, and social security numbers. If a prophet is that gifted, then why not prophesy to as many people as possible? If you can see in the spirit that strongly, then utilize your prophetic gift to the maximum. Many of these prophetic words that use extremely private information, such as bank account numbers and so forth, are artificial. These types of words tend to bring more attention to the clay than the Potter. They originate from the flesh and produce carnal responses where emotion is mistaken for the anointing based on the person delivering the word. A great number of people mistake charisma for the anointing. Others misidentify a "personality" for the oil. This causes some to embrace a synthetic prophetic word based on the name behind it but reject an authentic word that comes from God. A prophetically carnal word is produced by the flesh and comes from a familiar spirit that spews falsehoods rather than God-inspired prophecy.

> *But he that prophesieth speaketh unto men to edifi-*
> *cation, and exhortation, and comfort* (1 Corinthians
> 14:3).

A true word received from Elohim is birthed by the Spirit and not by flesh. It comes directly from the Lord. One word is given for selfish reasons; the other is given with no motives except to edify, exhort, and comfort. Which would you rather have? I want the word of the Lord even if I don't particularly care for the message. Some people hear a prophetic word and only receive and embrace part of it—the part that they like. They cast the rest aside like discarded junk mail.

There is a major difference between receiving a word and embracing it when it comes to the prophetic. You might receive a word, but did you embrace it? By definition, *receive* means to get or be given something. *Embrace* means to hold close with the arms, usually as an expression of affection. Can you see the difference here? Some prophetic words are given, but not all are held close. The ones that are held with affection or love usually stay with a person longer than prophetic words that are merely given. Some prophecies have stayed with me for years because I embraced them. I held on to these words because I loved them. I had affection for them because I knew that they came from God. An indicator that a prophecy comes from God is the love that lives within it. God is love according to First John 4:8, which states, *"He that loveth not knoweth not God, for God is love."* If God is love, then we can safely assume that His words are love as well. This can be the case when the prophecy is corrective as evidenced in Hebrews 12:6a: *"For whom the Lord loveth He chaseneth [corrects]."*

The main way God speaks today is through His prophets. Yes, many are prophets, but all are not His. Words can be sent to you through an oracle, but not every prophet comes from the Lord. The words spoken by them might be heard and received but should never be embraced. The false has a habit of coming before the true. You might receive some words but not necessarily love them. These types of words are often forgotten, but just like you'll never forget your first love, you won't forget the prophecies that originate from love.

Prophesying with Power

In my prophetic training sessions, I emphasize that the prophetic words that my students deliver should be accompanied by the power of God. When a word is delivered, it should be mighty enough to initiate change, internally and externally. If you decree a thing as a prophet, it should be established (see Job 22:28). I've made declarations and, in many cases, have seen them come to pass. That should be normal during prophecy. That's God's power working through prophetic words.

> *For the word of God is quick, and powerful, and sharper than any two-edged sword, piercing even to the dividing asunder of soul and spirit, and of the joints and marrow, and is a discerner of the thoughts and intents of the heart* (Hebrews 4:12).

Here we see that the word of God is quick, powerful, and sharp. *Quick* used in this Scripture means "living." This leads me to believe that the prophetic words coming from a prophet's mouth should be the same. When one speaks as an oracle of God, he or she speaks His words. The words that proceed out of the mouths of prophets should be alive, full of power, and sharper than any two-edged sword. They should penetrate to the point of dividing soul and spirit, joints and marrow; and judge the thoughts and attitudes of the heart (NIV). This is exactly what true prophetic utterances do. Whenever prophetic people speak in this manner, powerful, life-changing words result. All prophetic people should aspire to move to a level in God where their prophecies are accompanied by power and manifested decrees.

CHAPTER 6

Don't Have a Burger King Mentality!

*Teach me thy way, O Lord; I will
walk in thy truth: unite my heart to
fear thy name* (Psalm 86:11).

Most people are familiar with the fast-food giant Burger King. As a child, I can recall humming the jingles from their promotions. They used a catchy slogan that still exists today: "Have it your way!" Potential customers knew that if they went to Burger King, they could have food their way. The popular restaurant added, "Special orders don't upset us!" Some people of God have this mindset when it comes to prophetic ministry. They'll come to church, hoping to hear from God concerning a specific matter, but if the prophet doesn't address their particular concern during personal ministry, they become upset. Why? Because they didn't receive the word their way!

This has happened to me quite a few times. I've been 100 percent accurate, yet some will say, "I wanted a word concerning my husband, Harold," or "What about my job?" I can only give a person the word as God releases it His way, not my way. Early in my pastoral ministry, a woman wanted me to pray about her getting an apartment. I started to grant her request, but the Lord spoke to my spirit, telling me not to comply. In my desire to please her, I tried to pray for her apartment again. And again, I heard the same "no." I asked God why, and He replied that she had to correct some things in her life before He could fulfill her request. I took a deep breath and told her, as nicely as I could, the word of the Lord. She was not very happy about it. I went to the back, soaking wet after ministering to many people that night, and the host came in behind me. He stated that I needed to come with him immediately to speak with the same woman. I did and without going into too much detail, she again let me know her displeasure because I did not give her the word her way! Many people say that they want the truth, but most can't handle the truth once it's delivered. I'd rather hear godly honesty over demonic flattery.

> *Whoever rebukes a man will afterward find more favor than he who flatters with his tongue* (Proverbs 28:23 ESV).

While the truth might sting a bit at first, people usually appreciate it over time. I've told many a friend the truth regarding various situations only to be rebuffed for my candidness. Some years later, some of those same friends came back and apologized. Prophetic words might not always be polite, but sometimes they rudely awaken God's purpose and destiny resting in your spirit. Paul also had a habit of speaking the truth. He did so in reference to Peter acting one way with the Jews and another way with the Gentiles.

> *But when Peter came to Antioch, I had to oppose him to his face, for what he did was very wrong. When he first arrived, he ate with the Gentile believers, who were not circumcised. But afterward, when some friends of James came, Peter wouldn't eat with the Gentiles anymore. He was afraid of criticism from these people who insisted on the necessity of circumcision. As a result, other Jewish believers followed Peter's hypocrisy, and even Barnabas was led astray by their hypocrisy. When I saw that they were not following the truth of the gospel message, I said to Peter in front of all the others, "Since you, a Jew by birth, have discarded the Jewish laws and are living like a Gentile, why are you now trying to make these Gentiles follow the Jewish traditions?"* (Galatians 2:11-14 NLT)

Paul told Peter the truth as he saw it! Peter was acting hypocritically out of fear to the point that others followed suit. Much of the time, people are creatures of habit. They tend to follow the majority and the path of least resistance rather than the minority. I so admire Daniel in Scripture. He dared to be different, praying honestly to God with the window open three times a day, despite the decree of an ungodly king. He, like Paul, publicly acknowledged truth in spite of the dire consequences. When you stand on truth, God will back you. When you lie, Satan becomes a constant companion. He's the father of lies. He's not only the father of falsehoods, but he and his demons reside in each lie told! Once you tell one, others will follow. Many can handle the truth in regard to others but not to themselves. They will praise God with all their might in church as the preacher comes down hard on sin in general, but the praises stop when he or she points out their individual sin. Personally, I would rather hear the truth than an inflated lie. If the truth is spoken in love, it should be received in that same way. Sadly, the truth makes more enemies than it does friends. Paul knew this well as evidenced in Galatians 4:16: *"Am I therefore become your enemy because I tell you the truth?"*

People who have a "Burger King" mentality are usually the ones who don't want it God's way but want it their own way. They can be very selfish and spoiled in terms of their relationship with the Most High. It's usually all about them. The Lord is not a "have-it-your-way" God. It's His way or no way. In fact, followers of Jesus Christ were also called followers of "the Way." Our Lord and Savior stated in John 14:6, *"I am the way, the truth and the life: no man cometh to the Father, but by me."* Not only is He the way, but to get to the Father, we must do it His way. This means saying what He says, no matter the outcome. Some people will hate a prophet just because he or she didn't say what they wanted to hear.

Micaiah was such a prophet. *"So the king of Israel said to Jehoshaphat, 'There is still one man, Micaiah the son of Imlah, by whom we may inquire of the Lord: but I hate him, because he does not prophesy good concerning me, but evil'"* (1 Kings 22:8 NKJV). And Jehoshaphat said, *"Let not the king say such things!"*

Prior to this statement by the king of Israel, Jehoshaphat, the king of Judah, went to visit him, and Ahab asked if he would fight with him at Ramoth Gilead. Jehoshaphat agreed, but on the condition that the king of Israel would inquire of the Lord before entering battle. Ahab gathered four hundred prophets and asked them whether or not they should go into battle. All of them told him that he should go and that he would win. This, according to the prophets, was the word of the Lord. Jehoshaphat asked the king of Israel if there was another prophet of the Lord of whom he could inquire. Verse 8 provides the answer—Ahab expressed his hatred of Micaiah because of previous unfavorable prophecies toward him. In First Kings 22:13, the messenger who was sent to find Micaiah advised him to say what the other four hundred prophets said and encourage the king of Israel. Sometimes, prophets can focus so much on encouragement that they alter the word from the Lord. After hearing this, Micaiah was determined to speak whatever God told him, but when he arrived, he said exactly what the other prophets said. As prophetic people, we are called to be in the minority, not the majority, whether we like it or not. Many bow to peer pressure and deliver carnally inspired words rather than the words of God. We must have the boldness of Daniel in times when we are called to speak truth to those in power. Prophets must dare to be different.

As the chapter continues, Micaiah is pressed by the king to speak the truth, and he does. He tells Ahab that he will be defeated in battle—in fact, not just defeated but killed. The Lord told Micaiah that He put a lying spirit in the mouth of all of

Ahab's prophets and declared disaster against him. What a word! Though fear might have caused the prophet to initially lie, the truth bubbled up and came forth out of him when pressed. Please understand that whatever's in you will come out when pressure is applied. The truth was in Micaiah, and that's what came out. Later on, in First Kings 22, the prophecy was fulfilled; the King of Israel died, and the dogs licked up his blood while the harlots bathed.

We need more Micaiahs in the church today. We need prophets who will stand against the majority, finding comfort in the minority. These include seers who will release a word of "thus saith the Lord" without reservation, timidity, or fear. We need prophets who will speak the truths released from the heart and mind of God without thought of how this will affect their fame or ministerial relationships. We need prophets who will cry loud and spare not when it comes to injustice in and out of the church. We need seers who will speak the truth to power. These prophets are essentially the *dabar* of God, authoritative voices who are not afraid to speak courageously to those in authority (Strong's #H1697). God is raising up men and women in this hour who will not hold back prophecy in the presence of greatness. Elijah the prophet didn't withhold the Lord's message when he spoke to King Ahab. Instead of being timid, he released it with *exousia* (authority, Strong's #G1849) and *dunamis* (power, Strong's #G1411) in the following Scripture.

> *And Elijah the Tishbite, who was of the inhabitants of Gilead, said unto Ahab, As the Lord God of Israel liveth, before whom I stand, there shall not be dew nor rain these years, but according to my word. And*

*the word of the Lord came unto him, saying, Get thee
hence, and turn thee eastward, and hide thyself by the
brook Cherith, that is before Jordan* (1 Kings 17:1-3).

Elijah might have experienced fear when speaking to powerful
people, but he didn't let fear keep his mouth closed. Fear is one of
the biggest obstacles to the prophetic. I have seen so many prophetically gifted people paralyzed by fear that the word of the Lord is
continuously stuck in their throat, never exiting their lips. In the
spirit, I saw the enemy placing his grimy hands over the mouths
of prophets when they tried to give utterance to the bubbling
forth (*nabi*) that was seeking release from their bellies (Strong's
#H5030). Micaiahs won't have this problem. I decree that the
Micaiahs are arising in this hour. They will be nourished by the
Obadiahs (protectors and nurturers of prophets) of the last generation if only they're willing to listen and be equipped. In First Kings
18:4, Obadiah the prophet hid one hundred prophets from Jezebel
in caves and fed them with bread and water. If you are a Micaiah,
take heart! Your Obadiah is at hand to protect and nurture you.

Being a Micaiah sometimes means being without human company. However, they understand that in those situations, they're
never truly alone. God is always with them. Furthermore, God is
pleased that Micaiahs haven't let popularity rule His pronounce-
ments over their lives.

CHAPTER 7

The Timing of Prophetic Words

A man hath joy by the answer of his mouth:
and a word spoken in due season [time],
how good is it! (Proverbs 15:23).

I want to concentrate on the second part of the verse above, *"a word spoken in due season." Season* here means time. Prophetic words might be true but given out of season (time). Sometimes, the word prophesied is not meant to be released until a later date. I've seen a number of people misguided by ill-timed prophetic words. These types of words end up blocking destiny instead of propelling the hearer forward. Words given out of season can derail a person's destiny. They're very likely to walk into something they're unprepared for due to a lack of experience and wisdom.

At times, I released a prophetic word too early, and the person wasn't ready for it. When this happens, demonic activity increases in the recipient's life. The attacks intensify because of the prophetic words that were released. I've seen this many times and have learned to release what God says to release and keep what the Lord says to keep. Immature prophetic people sometimes believe that you're supposed to release *every* word that God gives you. Not true! At times, God would have you pray it rather than say it. In other words, you might be prophesying to a person when suddenly you see something terrible, such as illness, death, etc. The words of a prophet of God establish things and carry great weight. They have a tendency to manifest. As prophetic people, we must ask the Lord for permission to release these words during these times. The Lord might say, "No, I want you to pray it, not say it."

Prayer can be an extremely powerful tool to alter the person's present situation. In fact, it's one of the most neglected tools in the believer's arsenal! We must remember, prayer changes things, but prophecy has the ability to reset what has been changed. When you give prophetic words from the Lord, the person might receive a fresh start or outlook. This may confirm changes recently garnered through prayer and realign attitudes concerning faith. This will help them when receiving prayer concerning life-altering situations that the prophet did not address. We must always be the Master's mouthpiece, willing to speak or hold back as He commands. Words shouldn't be spoken based on chronological time but on the Lord's time. Please make sure you're on God's *kairos* (His time, Strong's #G2540) and not your *chronos* (your chronological time, Strong's #G5550) when releasing His word. Isaiah 50:4 tells us, *"The Lord God hath given me the tongue of the learned, that I should know how to speak a word in season to him that is weary: he wakeneth morning by morning, he wakeneth mine ear to hear as the learned."* In order to say what He wants us to say, we must be able to recognize His voice.

Once we know God's voice, we're able to discern His timing. Don't be surprised when the Lord shows you something about someone and then tells you not to release it at that time. Believe me, this happens more often than you think. I've admonished novice prophets when they tell every anointed or gifted person they see that they're apostles. This type of behavior is very common in today's church. I'm called an apostle on an almost daily basis. Peers have rebuked me for not accepting this word. My philosophy has always been to do the work, and people will call you what they see you do. That's what Jesus did. He never once focused on a title. He let His deeds speak for Him as should we. In this case, actions speak much louder than words. I'd rather see what you do than hear you talk about your credentials.

Words Can Hurt You!

The saying, "sticks and stones may break my bones, but words will never hurt me" reportedly first appeared in the March 1862 issue of *The Christian Recorder*, a publication of the African Methodist Episcopal Church.[1] However, this popular adage is only partially true. Yes, sticks and stones have the latent power to break and harm, depending on who is wielding both, but words do, too. Proverbs 18:21 tells us that the power of life and death is in the tongue. Words can hurt you.

When allowing people to minister to you, be very careful about what you permit them to speak into your spirit. I've learned to not allow demoniacally disguised information to enter into my ear gates, whether or not the speaker realizes what he or she is saying. When they begin to minister verbally to me, I will immediately stop them when I feel the words are of satanic origin. I want to emphasize that the speaker might not know this, but when you discern it, you must end the conversation or make the person stop their evil report.

We have a radio broadcast called "Faith to Endure" that comes on WBGX AM 1570 (The Big Gospel Express) Monday through Friday at 7:15 a.m. CST as of the publishing of this book. Years ago, a woman heard me on the show and decided to call to discuss specific services that she could offer our church. In the midst of our dialogue, she suddenly broke forth in unknown tongues very loudly. Each time she did it, my spirit was immensely grieved as it just didn't sound right. I could sense from the tone of her voice when she spoke in the spirit (tongues) that she might be a witch on assignment. The tongues that emanated from her mouth were not of God. At that point, I ended the call and haven't heard from her since. The enemy has a distinct sound, which you have to be able to discern as the person speaks.

In Acts 16, the woman with the spirit of divination (*python,* Strong's 4436) said all the right things but with the wrong spirit or motivation. Paul identified the motivation behind the words and rebuked it. The woman then lost her "gift" and her master's gain. Do not receive everything whispered in your ear or spoken through your cellphone or released on social media in this season. Instead, stop them mid-sentence and let them know that you are not receiving what they're dishing out. You cannot eat from everyone's table, especially if the meal has a past history of not agreeing with you.

Note

1.   Gary Martin, "Sticks and Stones May Break My Bones," Phrasefinder, accessed March 27, 2018, http://www.phrases.org .uk/meanings/sticks-and-stones-may-break-my-bones.html.

CHAPTER 8

The Prophetic Mindset

*Let this mind be in you, which was also
in Christ Jesus* (Philippians 2:5).

A prophetic mind is a mind that hears, discerns, predicts, and reveals what the Lord thinks, feels, and communicates to the earth."[1] Every Holy-Ghost-filled believer should have this mind and maintain it. One of the reasons that some don't operate fully in the prophetic is because they do not have a prophetic mind. If you have the mind of Christ, then you will also have a prophetic mindset. The word *let* used in Philippians 2:5 means "to allow or permit." We must allow or permit the mentality of Christ to flow through us before we can have His mind.

Many are resistant to the prophetic mindset due to ignorance concerning the prophetic. They have encountered so many false prophets that they are unable to recognize the true ones. Mistrust, anxiety, fear, and apprehension are the governing spirits of those who have been embattled in ungodly prophetic assaults, for example, a barrage of false prophecies one after another. Some avoid prophetic gatherings because of negative experiences with the prophetic. This has led some leaders to overly regulate prophetic activity in their churches. First Peter 5:3 explains that we should not lord over (dominate) God's heritage (people), but being examples to the flock. As leaders, we're not to prod people as we would cattle but lead them as God's sheep. Second Corinthians 3:17 lets us know that where the spirit of the Lord is, there is liberty. In my opinion, there is not only liberty, but there is also prophecy. Some use the prophetic to enslave, not liberate. Without a prophetic mindset, the gift of prophecy might be used as a gimmick to gain popularity, finances, acceptance, and allegiance by the uninformed. When you lack a prophetic mind, words meant to be prophetic are often infected with confusion.

First Corinthians 14:33 says, *"For God is not [the author] of confusion, but of peace, as in all churches of the saints."* I refer to this Scripture to emphasize that people might prophesy but lack the mindset and proper gift development, which causes the prophecy to be uttered from double-mindedness and instability. James 1:8 admonishes that a double-minded man is unstable in all his ways.

Historically bad experiences with the prophetic can cause leaders with an underdeveloped prophetic mindset to become so overprotective of their sheep that true prophetic flow is blocked in their churches. True prophetic ministry gifts won't be invited because of prophetic prejudice built on ignorance. Untrained and unused prophetic mechanics lead to faulty prophetic mindsets. According to noted author Dr. Paula Price, "Remedies must begin where obstacles formed."[2] One of Satan's favorite targets is our mind as this is where he establishes his roadblocks. If he can access your mind, then he can disrupt or derail your destiny. Don't give him any permission to enter your mind. Instead, walk according to Romans 12:2, which says, *"And be not conformed to this world: but be ye transformed by the renewing of your mind, that ye may prove what is that good, and acceptable, and perfect, will of God."*

We must renew our minds through the testimony of Jesus, which is the spirit (life) of prophecy, according to Revelation 19:10. Prophetic words have the innate ability to renew. In Revelation 21:5a, Jesus said that He makes all things new. When you have a new mindset, you will speak new words. Jesus had this type of mindset. First Corinthians 2:16 tells us, *"For who hath known the mind of the Lord, that he may instruct him? but we have the mind of Christ."* When you have a prophetic mindset and speak prophetically, you are literally causing the mind of God to become audible within the earth.

If you don't have a prophetic mindset, you will struggle to become adept or skilled in the prophetic. This is why some churches can't see the need for prophecy because their vision is clouded by tradition. We must see through the Father's eyes instead of our own. Remember, you see with your mind through your eyes. The prophetic mindset will cause your spiritual vision or prophetic sight to become clearer. Hebrews 8:10 states that God writes His laws in our hearts and minds.

When we encounter resistance to the prophetic, then we can administer prophetic therapy. Therapy is defined as the treatment of a mental disorder. The lack of a prophetic mindset is a spiritual disorder that affects one mentally. This leads us right into my next topic—prophetic therapy.

Notes

1. Dr. Paula Price, Spoken message at Antioch Church, Joliet, IL, August 20, 2016.

2. Dr. Paula Price, *Prophecy: God's Divine Communications Media*, (Tulsa: Flaming Vision Publications, 2003).

CHAPTER 9

Prophetic Therapy

And Jesus answering said unto them,
They that are whole need not a physician;
but they that are sick (Luke 5:31).

When you are sick in your body, you should logically and reasonably see a physician. What about when you are sick within your spirit? Who do you see when you need spiritual healing? Many of the infirmities within the body are caused by the demonic realm and need to be addressed by a specialist in the things of the spirit. Prophets of God are such specialists and are integral to the healing and restoration of the body. By nature, prophets have a divine ability to "see" the revelations of God pertaining to the complaint of the inquirer, such as sickness. At times, I have seen afflicted parts of the body while prophesying before the person tells me about the problem. The prophetic allows you to see what sickness is troubling a person, the reason behind it, and the recipe for healing. In many instances, you do not need to let a *true* prophet know what ails you. He or she should be able to discern it and provide a remedy. Nothing is more disgraceful than a man or woman of God who prophetically verbalizes information about a specific sickness without an accompanying prayer and impartation of healing.

Prophets are healers. When done properly, a prophet should be able to diagnose the condition and decree the healing into manifestation. Prophets are the mouthpieces of the Most High. God can and will speak healing through His prophets. *"He sent His word and healed them"* (Ps. 107:20). When God sends a word, it falls into the mouth of those with a prophetic edge, an ear to hear what the Spirit of God is saying. It is pronounced to the people, and they are healed. The Word given is Jesus because He is the Word of God (see John 1:1,14). He is also the Holy Spirit that resides in every believer (see Eph. 1:13). A prophetic person can prophesy healing because the Word (Jesus) dwells inside them. God speaks to their spirit, and their spirit translates His word in a way that personally connects with them. His servant makes decrees regarding what the Holy Ghost has put into his or her mouth concerning specific healing or deliverance. Your own healing is encompassed within the realm of the prophetic. Healing is in the mouth of the prophet and is manifested through God-inspired, spoken words.

Prophetic therapy is the treatment of any illness or disorder through a combination of discernment, a word of knowledge, word of wisdom, and prophecy. All four of these are part of the nine gifts of the Spirit mentioned in First Corinthians 12:8-16. They are used respectively to diagnose, treat, and cure spiritual sickness. First, the *word of knowledge* identifies the problem and provides information concerning the root cause, such as generational curses, sin, etc. For example, in Acts 16:16-18 when Paul dealt with the damsel with the spirit of divination, he proffered a word of knowledge pertaining not to what the woman was saying but to the spirit behind the words. Hosea 4:6 reminds us that we can be destroyed due to a lack of knowledge. Second, a *word of wisdom* helps the recipient understand the what, why, where, and how of an adverse spiritual situation that has manifested in the natural as sickness. It presents a supernatural solution to a supernatural issue. For example, in First Kings 3:16-28, Solomon exhibited wisdom when addressing a situation when two mothers fought over one baby. In Second Kings 3:15-16, Elisha received a word of wisdom that instructed him to make a valley full of ditches. Third, prophecy is an inspired utterance of a prophet or a prophetic person. This is the will of the Lord in a particular situation.

Prophetic therapy is sorely needed in the Body of Christ today. They that neglect it do so at their own peril. A major aspect of this therapy is discernment, which is the heightened ability to hear, read, or consider a proposed course of action and determine whether the source is human, demonic, or divine. You also need to identify spirits of infirmity through this vehicle (see John 8:15-16; Heb. 4:12). Judgment is an essential part of discernment. "Judge not" as mentioned in Matthew 7:1 refers to a hypocritical type of judgment instead of divine judgment. First Corinthians 5:3,12 admonishes us to judge those inside the house of God, and

Jesus will judge those outside. First Corinthians 6:2-3 lets us know that we will judge angels. So why is it wrong for a Christian to judge? In short, it's not! The spirit in which we judge makes all the difference.

In Matthew 16:16-17, 22-23, Jesus spoke of the revelation that Peter, His disciple, received from Father God. In the next verses, Peter rebuked Jesus, and Jesus then rebuked the devil that was influencing the words of Peter. Jesus understood who was speaking to Him at that moment, and it wasn't Peter. The enemy took over his flesh, inspiring the words that came from Peter's mouth. The enemy will come for your words right after the birthing of a revelation from God. We must use the gift of discernment to comprehend who and what is speaking to us or through us. Paul did this when confronted with the damsel. What Peter and the damsel said wasn't necessarily wrong in the natural, but it was definitely a no-no in the spirit. We must use discernment to see behind the words that are spoken. Many say things that seem right in the natural, but they are not accurate in the spirit. You can tell the truth, but the truth might not have been the right thing to say in a particular situation, especially when it could cause discord among the brethren. There is a season for everything, even the spoken word. First John 4:1 admonishes us to test the spirit to see if it is of God. In order to test the spirit, you must first discern the spirit.

CHAPTER 10

Prophetic Etiquette

Let all things be done decently and in
order (1 Corinthians 14:40).

Holy Words Given with Unholy Breath

I've discussed spiritually polluted prophecies, so now I'll address the naturally polluted prophecy. If a prophet or prophetic person's breath is foul, his/her prophetic words will more than likely be foul as well. I've experienced that many times, when the breath was rancid, the prophecy was off. I'm not talking about the breath being a little tart. I'm referring to a putrid odor that you can smell six feet before you reach a person. I'm also not referring to bad breath caused by illness. I'm talking about a basic lack of hygiene that causes a person's breath to smell like a demon. After all, devils are called unclean for a reason. The kind of smell I'm referring to is one that is so bad that you consider taking the person through deliverance. I have seen a correlation here too many times for it to be a coincidence. I want you to *selah* on this one (Strong's #H5542). Have you ever received a prophetic word that was 100 percent accurate from someone whose breath was kicking? Stop laughing because I'm serious! Check your hygiene, especially if you work in close proximity with others. I taught this during a prophetic activation class, and a multitude of people ran up to grab breath mints from near the altar.

Respect the Dignity of Those to Whom You Minister

When you have an extremely personal word from the Lord for someone in a prophetic line, don't say it loud enough for anyone else to hear. Instead, just whisper the words in the person's ear in order to protect their privacy and dignity.

Don't Compete During Prophecy!

When you prophesy with other prophets, don't try to prophetically "show off" as better than all the other prophets before you. The ministry of the prophetic is not a competition. Instead, focus on the word that God has for the person and not on other prophets.

The Danger of Asking a Lot of Questions During Personal Prophecy

We've touched on this briefly, but I want to expand on this further. Whenever possible, I advise people not to ask any questions during prophetic ministry. It's a recipe for disaster. When you are just starting to move in your prophetic gift, it's somewhat understandable to ask questions. However, if you have to ask twenty questions while you're giving someone a personal prophecy, it's a sure sign that you're a novice. When you ask questions, you are setting yourself up to give false prophecies. You're allowing the questions, not God, to dictate the direction and shape of your prophetic words. Never do this. Instead of hearing from God, you're hearing from the person to whom you're prophesying. The person you're questioning might be lying. Your "prophetic" responses were predicated on deceptive replies, not on the authentic truth that comes only from the Lord. Don't use questions as a measuring stick of the direction you should take prophetically.

An apostle once made a bold statement to my church that if you depend on questions to prophesy, you're a beginner. This hit me like a ton of bricks because I had ministered for her a couple of months earlier and had done just that—asked questions while prophesying. My first response was one of offense. How dare she come into my church and throw shade at me? But as I thought about it, she was right. Though this was years ago, her words still reverberate today. I learned a valuable lesson that night. This is one of the main reasons that I make statements instead of inquiries when personally ministering to people. When you make statements that God actually spoke to you, you won't have to worry about accuracy; you'll have exactness. You will be 100 percent exact instead of just 50 percent accurate.

In stating that, I'm very concerned with the lack of training among many so-called prophets of God. Many are "prophelying" instead of prophesying and messing up a whole lot of lives. Prophetic words are weighty and should not be shared lightly. If you have to literally interrogate people in order to give them a word, then you probably need a bit more training before prophesying to the nations.

The Spirit Behind that Prophetic Word You Received

A prophetic word should not always refer to tangible things but to intangibles that specifically direct the person into who they're called to be in God. If the word given is always about a new home, car, wealth, the downfall of your enemies, your haters, etc., then that word is likely rooted in carnality and not spirituality. It's probably tied to the natural and not the supernatural. Please remember that all spirituality is not godly. All prophecy is not from God, such as words from the prophets of Baal and others, but the origin might be camouflaged as godliness. When prophetic words overemphasize flesh, it's a sign to check the source of those words. The woman with the spirit of divination or python spirit in Acts 16 spoke accurate words to Paul and his comrades. She made much gain for her masters through the utterance of correct prophetic words of knowledge, such as a psychic would. While she was right in terms of her words, she was speaking from the wrong source—Satan. As soon as Paul cast the devil out of her, she lost her prophetic ability. As I've stated before, Romans 11:29 says the gifts and callings of God are without repentance. The Lord will not take back the gift(s) that He's given you, but Lucifer will. The next time that you receive a prophetic word that overemphasizes your natural self above your spiritual self, check the source. Selah.

Part III

THE PROPHET

CHAPTER 11

The Importance of the Prophetic Office

Now therefore restore the man his wife; for
he is a prophet, and he shall pray for thee,
and thou shalt live (Genesis 20:7a).

Prophets can't take other prophets to realms where they are only visitors. They can only take them to realms where they are residents. In order to mantle a prophet, you must be a prophet. Throughout the Old Testament, senior prophets produced, trained, and sent out other prophets. As with any apostolic gift, you should be able to reproduce what you are. For example, if you're a senior leader of a church and a prophet, prophets should be coming out of your church. Your church should have prophetic presbytery, trainings, and strategies for thrusting them out into the world.

The importance of the prophetic office cannot be denied. In fact, the very world we live in was birthed through the prophetic words of the Most High. God spoke the words "let there be" throughout the thirty-one verses of the first chapter of Genesis. Everything that exists finds its origin in the prophetic and in the mouths of the prophets.

Genesis 20:7 refers to Abraham when it says, *"He is a prophet."* He was the first person to be identified in Scripture as a prophet but not the first prophet in biblical history. Luke 11:50-51 explains who this prophet was. *"That the blood of all the prophets, which was shed from the foundation of the world, may be required of this generation; from the blood of Abel unto the blood of Zacharias, which perished between the altar and the temple: verily I say unto you, It shall be required of this generation."*

Based upon the Scriptures above, Abel was the first prophet. Abel never spoke any words of prophecy recorded in the Bible, yet he's referred to by Jesus as a prophet. Other prophets in the Bible also never recorded one prophetic word but were still referred to as prophets. As previously mentioned in Chapter 6, in First Kings 18:4, Obadiah the prophet hid one hundred prophets from Jezebel in caves and fed them with bread and water. None of these prophets were recorded as speaking a single word in Scripture, yet they're still identified as prophets.

Let me again make a clear distinction here. Just because one has the ability to prophesy does not mean that person is a prophet.

As mentioned earlier in this book, there's a difference between the *gift* of prophecy and the *office* of a prophet. Prophets have the ability to release mantles, symbolizing the passing down of a person's ministry to another, many times in a greater measure. Those with prophetic abilities who do not walk in the office of a prophet cannot release mantles. Second Kings 2:11-14 further demonstrates this as the mantle is passed from Elijah to his servant Elisha. Elijah dropped the mantle as he was taken up by God in a whirlwind of fire, and Elisha was there to pick it up. Bible experts report that Elisha served Elijah between six and twelve years before receiving his mantle. After receiving the mantle, Elisha had a successful prophetic ministry for sixty to sixty-five years. Before Elijah's ascension, Elisha asked for a double portion of Elijah's spirit in Second Kings 2:9-10. He received the answer to his request because he was in the right place at the right time. Because of his servanthood, faithfulness, and tenacity, Elisha was mantled for his mandate as a prophet.

This is also true today. In order to use any gift, you must be instructed in its proper use. Elisha was trained by Elijah. This method of biblical prophetic discipleship should be adhered to today. As I've already touched on, one of the best individuals to train up a prophet is another prophet. Check the Scriptures for yourself. In the Old Testament, novice prophets were trained by seasoned prophets, not by other gifts or offices, in schools specifically for that purpose. Today, we have everyone and their mothers giving prophetic trainings, but true impartation, education, and activation comes through an instructor with an established prophetic gifting and ministry.

Prophets can lack structure and seem a bit unorganized. When they minister, they don't always stick to their outlines. They usually have a strong proclivity to preach prophetically, going off script and allowing the Lord to dictate His message to them while delivering the spoken word. Prophetic personalities have a tendency to openly rebuke, use sharp words, correct, call out, speak brutal truth in love, expose sin, stir up, thrust out, reproduce, impart, activate, detonate, educate, eradicate, and emancipate.

CHAPTER 12

A Process Is Attached to Your Calling

Now for this very reason also, applying all diligence, in your faith supply moral excellence, and in your moral excellence, knowledge; and in your knowledge, self-control, and in your self-control, perseverance, and in your perseverance, godliness; and in your godliness, brotherly kindness, and in your brotherly kindness, love (2 Peter 1:5-7 NASB).

Let me expand upon what I've previously written in this book. Prophetic people today have a strong tendency to prophesy gifts, titles, and callings. While this is not impossible, a word must be given in the right season (time). For example, a prophet might tell someone that they're called to be an apostle, but the recipient has demonstrated little evidence of this based on historical behavior and character. Past behavior is a strong indicator of future behavior. If a person has been chronically tardy for his or her job for years, then such behavior will most likely persist. When indicating that you see someone as this or that in the future, you should be able to glimpse some evidence of the godly assignment within current behavior. If the person responds with complacency or disinterest, maybe that person was not prepared to receive that word at that particular time. As I've previously mentioned, I've seen many receive a word out of season, and the enemy wreaked havoc in their lives afterward. Satan attacks them because he is afraid of the possible manifestation of the prophetic declaration in their lives.

The Lord has a pattern of promoting the faithful. He hasn't changed. He's the same today, yesterday, and forever. The word given concerning your call should resound in your spirit. This should happen even if you question the word initially. People regularly told my mother that I was going to be a preacher. My reaction to that was absolutely not! I had no interest whatsoever in a life of ministry. However, as I grew older, I had dreams of speaking to large groups of people. I felt the pulling of God and experienced His protection throughout my formative years. Others saw what I was called to be in my haste to escape it. Something on the inside of me knew that what they were saying regarding ministry was true. We must always realize that we're only here to accomplish God's will. When we surrender to this, His will becomes our will.

In John 14:11, Jesus said, *"Believe me that I am in the Father, and the Father in me: or else believe me for the very works' sake."* Our Lord did the work regardless of whether or not people believed in Him. The miracles or work Jesus performed spoke volumes long before those closest to Him knew who He truly was. What you do for God has a sound that can be heard by others before you walk in the call. The work always precedes the call. You will usually see signs that God has called someone to a certain gifting/office.

I want to again repeat the following: people sometimes demonstrate prophetic irresponsibility within the Body of Christ. In other words, a prophet might release a word that was not for that specific season. Many today misinterpret an anointing for a gifting or office, which is why we have so many so-called apostles in the Body of Christ who are actually in the wrong office. They fail to demonstrate God's power. Throughout Scripture, God qualified those He called through processes, meaning they had to go through some difficult things before they were elevated to greater authority. Examples include Joseph, Moses, David, Jesus, and others. We have so many who want the office/gifting without the process. This is a main reason that some are ill-equipped for leadership. This is why there's an influx of the apostolic/prophetic offices but a decline of the pastoral, evangelistic, and teaching gifts. It's a sad commentary on life in the Body today.

If you can't faithfully attend your local church services, then how will you believe a prophetic word that tells you that you're called to be an apostle to nations? Let me clarify this further: if you don't attend church regularly, a "prophetic word" that you're an apostle called to the nations might not be accurate. I have a hard time with that because your leadership should see some evidence of that call on your life before the word was given. There is a time for everything, even prophetic words. You must first answer the call (summon), go through the conditioning (process), and then you'll receive the commissioning (mandate).

As I've mentioned previously, a word like that can bring unnecessary demonic attack on some who may not be ready for such an onslaught. When I first came into agreement with the prophetic call on my life all hell broke loose, literally! In December of 2008 I reached out to author, prophet, and prayer warrior Ruth Brown, who later became my spiritual mother, regarding the prophetic office and my place in it. We spoke via telephone and, after seeing a picture of me on our church website, she stated that I was a mighty prophet of God. With that confirmation and others, I scheduled an affirmation service with prophetic presbytery in attendance for March 17, 2009. Little did I know that by accepting the office of the prophet, the hordes of hell would attack me as never before!

On January 20, 2009, my biological mother suddenly died. A couple of days after her passing, my uncle was found dead in his basement from a massive heart attack. Within the next couple of months, we discovered our beloved family dog dead at the top of the stairs when we arrived home from church. Later that same year, my grandfather died. I dealt with a major illness and lost many of our church members. 2009 was the most devastating year of my life! I have never experienced anything like it before or since and pray I never will again.

My experience demonstrates how the enemy will target you when you start heading in the direction of your destination. The devil is already fearful of you being saved, but when you start walking toward your calling, he panics! Why? Because that's when you truly become a threat to his kingdom. In his panic, he won't just attack you but those you hold dear, including family and friends. He fights dirty! I've seen many of God's chosen ones go through worse situations than mine. These demonically inspired assaults were orchestrated by the enemy of our souls, who will stop at nothing to prevent us from evolving into who the Lord has called us to be.

One characteristic of the devil I've noticed over the years and find to be very encouraging is that he fights hard but not long. This should let you know that what you're currently going through has an expiration date. His strategic attacks against us usually occur in spurts or for specific periods of time. This is why I advise emerging leaders to make their calling and election sure. There's nothing worse than going through tremendous adversity for an office/gift that wasn't ordained by the Lord. Be totally convinced that God has called you to this office because you will have to pay a price for the oil/anointing of God attached to every gift He gives.

Proverbs 15:23 further explains this concept. *"A man hath joy by the answer of his mouth: and a word spoken in due season, how good is it!"* A word spoken in God's time (*kairos*) is a beneficial word. A word spoken in our time (*chronos*) can be a hurtful word. When we replace the *kairos* of God with the *chronos* of man, we short-circuit God's timing. All prophecy should be divinely inspired, not man-made. No matter how deep you are, even if you're a continuous visitor to the third, fourth, or seventh heaven, God will never show you *everything* about the person to whom you're prophesying.

I prophesied as a kid, knowing nothing about my call as a prophet. If you just "play" church and aren't educated on your calling by a seasoned minister, you aren't building on the right foundation. I'm not saying that a ministry of this type will never be effective. I'm just saying it's not likely, and many of these individuals end up being unprepared leaders. When we're faithful over *few things*, then God will make us ruler over *much*. This principle doesn't work in reverse.

Life has a natural and spiritual order to it. For example, you work a secular job. You're on time, have great attendance, and are a team player. The boss promotes you, which is well deserved. Now let's look at an example in church. You have poor attendance. When you do come, you're always late. You never help out. You refuse to submit to God or church leadership. You should have no reason to think the pastor or God will promote you. You shouldn't think that you could go to church and do nothing, have no academic requirements, work any way you want, not be able to sing if you're on the praise-and-worship team, only know three Scriptures, and still be qualified for a leadership position.

Prophetic Irresponsibility

As mentioned earlier, a process is attached to developing your calling and also releasing words that launch others into their purpose. A prophetic word, at its best, produces life, but some prophetic words produce death. How does something divinely inspired cause destruction? It does so mainly through flawed timing. You have a prophetic responsibility to ensure that you don't release words irresponsibly, including giving a word not meant for that specific season.

CHAPTER 13

Encouragement for Misfit Prophets

*But ye are a chosen generation, a royal
priesthood, an holy nation, a peculiar
people; that ye should shew forth the praises
of him who hath called you out of darkness
into his marvelous light* (1 Peter 2:9).

Wilderness Prophets

While prophets often struggle to fit in, some will face greater challenges than the average seer. This may cause them to seek shelter in the isolation of the wilderness. You are a wilderness prophet if you are trained with little to no outside help from man. Much of the wilderness experience encompasses what you go through on your way to prophetic maturity. This is the sum of your experiences and the wisdom that you have gleaned from them. Man cannot take the credit for your education during these times because God has essentially prepared and equipped you to walk in your prophetic calling.

Jesus didn't do any recorded miracles until after His time in the wilderness where God sent Him to be tempted by the enemy (see Matt. 4:1-11). In your wilderness, you will be tested. After you've passed varied examinations and gone through the harshness of the wild, then and only then will you be able to walk in the prophetic power that comes from God through experience.

Many novice or emerging prophets need to be taught the how, when, and where of prophecy. So many have the ability but haven't thoroughly read the instructions that came along with that same gift. I've seen this many times. They have the gift of prophecy, but don't know how to use it or are fearful of using it.

As I've addressed previously, Samuel established a school of prophets to train novice prophets in the prophetic and in the mandates of God. Being a prophet involves much more than just prophesying. That's only one component. Some prophets are trained by God in the wilderness; others are trained by senior prophets, and some are trained by life. Just like any other gift, you need education to properly use the prophetic gift.

I want to emphasize that your season in the wilderness is just that—a season. It's not meant to be permanent. You need to connect with mature prophets and those who can speak into your life. Do not allow yourself to become a Lone Ranger prophet, or you can quickly fall into error. Remember, even the Lone Ranger had Tonto.

Forgotten Prophets

True prophets will endure a season of being forgotten only to be remembered later in their kingly or God-ordained season. Someone will remember how they accurately prophesied to them and bring up their words to the king. The Lord will then release, bless, and promote them. We see this example in the life of Joseph. Don't be discouraged during this season but continue to be faithful to what God has shown you.

Topless Prophet

"Topless prophets" are seers with no covering, leaving them naked and exposed. Ephesians 5:23 spells out this concept, showing that covering does not necessarily refer just to marriage. The husband is the covering of the wife; Jesus is the covering of the church, and we know God is the head of Christ. As a Christian, God is your head. Let's not twist our understanding of covering. However, some "prophets" don't have a person or almighty God as their covering. This is a dangerous place from which to minister because if neither are their covering or head, the enemy will quickly fill the vacancy. Those "prophets" become prophetic unto themselves and become disqualified as an accurate mouthpiece of God. They receive information from a sensual realm instead of the throne room of the Most High. Money sometimes becomes their primary motivator instead of the mandates of God.

Don't be a "topless prophet." They go into warfare barely dressed and are sorely beaten due to a lack of proper covering. You will see a great benefit when someone more senior than yourself mentors you or spiritually parents and helps guide you along in ministry and life. Timothy did. Elisha did. Many in Scripture were assigned someone more experienced under whom they trained. In First Kings 19:16, God told Elijah to anoint Elisha to replace him. Your prophetic leader must always be thinking of the future. You must always be prepared to move into the position God has been preparing you for your whole life. God operates through relationships with others in similar callings, not through topless prophets. Always seek the Most High, and He will guide you to who He wants to train you. An ancient quote tells us, "When the student is ready, the teacher will appear." This is true within the prophetic realm. If you are an "Elisha" in need of an "Elijah" in your life, God will send him or her when you're ready. In the future, God will likely call you as an "Elijah" to your own "Elisha."

CHAPTER 14

Wrong Prophetic Motives

*Blessed are the pure in heart: for they
shall see God* (Matthew 5:8).

I love the prophetic, and I adore prophetic people. It's my mission
in life to help raise prophetic awareness and train leaders. I am
greatly disturbed by the utterances that are coming out of the
mouths of well-known prophetic leaders, words claiming to be
from the Lord. I just viewed a video from a famous prophet with
specific words and timings related to dates, world affairs, and the
like. This person gave specific words about twenty different topics
that failed to come to pass.

This is a blemish not only on the prophetic office but on prophetic people everywhere. These so-called prophets continue to falsely prophesy mainly because we don't hold them and their incorrect prophecies accountable. Why do we continue to flock to their conferences, send them money, and allow them to speak into our lives? If they give you a false word, why not let them know? Many people can't tell the difference between prophecy and guessing. You know the false ones because they'll use the prophetic to steal money from your pocket.

In 1999, I heard a prophet tell people to give $199.99, and he would give them a word; give $100, and he might speak a word to them; give $50, and he would "just" pray for them. This type of behavior is absolutely demonic! I rarely hear other leaders speak against these fraudulent actions because they're afraid of offending the person and taking heat from those who love the prophet. But what about offending God? If you receive money for a prophetic word, you're operating as a *psychic*, not a *prophet*. As a psychic, you'll still be right part of the time. As I've said, the devil always uses God's truth to establish his own lies. The enemy wants to trap you with partial truths. These words tend to become more "accurate" when the level of money given rises. If you prophesy for *profit*, then you're not a *prophet*. Yes, prophetic ministries need money, but the prophetic words given should not be for sale. Let the true, authentic prophets emerge in this hour to replace the false ones. I just heard God say that it's already begun! Thank you, Lord!

When I'm referring to inaccuracies and partial truths, I'm not referring to emerging prophets. People of God, emerging prophets will make mistakes, especially if they're not trained or mentored properly. For this reason, they must sit under seasoned prophets for a period of time (at least three years or more) in order to learn how to flow prophetically. We must always remember the importance of going through the prophetic process. Yes, prophets are born, but their gift is sharpened through discipleship. The more you go through the process, the keener your gift becomes.

Far too many emerging prophetic gifts are trained as armor bearers instead of disciples. They pick up the leader's laundry, walk their dogs, and wash their cars. This does very little in causing them to actualize the ministry with which God has entrusted them. I've seen people with great callings upon their lives languish in a church for twenty-plus years simply because the pastor refused to release them. A person should not have to be "released" from the house of the Lord but should just leave when they are so led. Prisoners are the only ones who come to mind when I think of people needing to be released.

Throughout my tenure as a lay member, I submitted to leadership yet maintained my own mind. God has given us a brain, and we should use it often. I thought for myself and refused to allow others to think for me or about me. Some have agendas that have very little to do with your call to ministry. If a leader has a church of thousands, in most cases he or she will not be able to hear God better than you do concerning your own life. Believers have the Holy Spirit for a reason. He teaches us, guides us, and comforts us regarding our journey in Him. Don't allow anyone to have a greater voice in your life than the Lord. If He's called you to prophetic ministry, heed the call or else you'll experience a lot of wasted years that could have been productive ones.

CHAPTER 15

How to Avoid Deception When Prophesying

For we ourselves also were sometimes foolish,
disobedient, deceived, serving divers lusts
and pleasures, living in malice and envy,
hateful, and hating one another. But after
that the kindness and love of God our Saviour
toward man appeared (Titus 3:3-4).

My experience as a prophetic trainer has afforded me many insights. Upcoming prophets need appropriate training, ongoing mentorship, and continued maturation of their gift. Correction is a very important part of prophetic oversight. I tell the members of my church that if I can't correct you, then I can't pastor you. It never ceases to amaze me how so many reject chastisement. Proverbs 3:12 says, *"For whom the Lord loveth he correcteth; even as a father the son in whom he delighteth."* A blessing lies in correction because He corrects those He loves. Prophets will give you what the Lord says, not what you want to hear. Nathan rebuked David in Second Samuel 12. It wasn't a pleasant word, but David received it. If you can endure discipline, then you will grow from it.

As a teenager, each time my heart was broken by a girl, I matured a bit. It's similar to hard words spoken to you by God. I've been in services where I've had to release words that some really did not want to hear. Some strongly expressed their dissatisfaction. I've had some leaders approach me with one or two complaints from their congregation. My response was always the same: I have to say what God instructs me to say, not what they want to hear. We have far too many prophets seeking to satiate people with prophecy instead of expressing the true heart of God. This is a mistake. I'm not saying that every word from the Lord should be harsh. However, every prophetic word that proceeds from your mouth should be divinely inspired by God, especially if you say, "thus saith the Lord" after every sentence.

In this world that's filled with false prophets and false prophecies, you can still go somewhere for an accurate word from the Lord—the Bible. The Word of God is always accessible, always authentic, always relevant, and you don't have pay a registration fee! To me, the Bible is a mirror. When you look in it, you should see yourself as you are and as you will be. What bothers me concerning novice or renegade prophets arising is the motivation behind their ascensions. Some are focused on making their own names great, which governs the topic of their prophetic proclamations regarding the nation. If they prophesy incorrectly multiple times about multiple subjects, we need to question honoring the gift within them just because they have a well-known name. I believe that we sometimes confuse loyalty to a personality with obedience to the Holy Spirit. When I speak for God, I must say what He says regardless of human offense, discomfort, or dislike. Why? Because that personality you love and honor so much might lead you straight to hell and make money on your descent.

Sometimes people can receive answers about so-called "maligned" prophets only if they come to a special meeting or conference or buy a book. This is nothing more than marketing at its finest. Many of these hirelings—I mean, prophets—have made money their god, no matter how loud or how long they say, *"Jesus!"* I am appalled at the state of the prophetic in this hour. Apostle John Eckhardt and many others have spent untold hours promoting its value while some have used it simply for monetary gain. In this season, God's sheep will identify these prophets of prostitution and use the authentic seers to eliminate the filthy lucre gained through those "Burger King" words I mentioned earlier. Be careful who you allow to speak into your life, swear allegiance to, or sow your seed into. You can rely on some true prophetic voices out there but don't put your trust in them. The only person you can trust in is God. Appropriately enough, the Bible reminds us of this very fact. *"It is better to trust in the Lord than to put confidence in man"* (Ps. 118:8). He will *never* market or prostitute His Word, and it will always be accurate.

CHAPTER 16

Prophets vs. Psychics

And Samuel grew, and the Lord was
with him, and did let none of his words
fall to the ground (1 Samuel 3:19).

Back in the early 1990s, before I was truly saved, I encountered a tarot card reader (psychic) at a nightclub in Chicago. I had just fallen out with my girlfriend and was in a really bad way. As I was walking, with no plans of seeing a psychic reader, one nearby called out to me. She was a short, older woman, dressed colorfully, sitting at a very tall and round table. The psychic's first words to me were, "She loves you! She doesn't love anybody else!" She immediately had my attention. I cautiously approached her table and took a seat.

This tarot card reader spread her cards across the table and began to "prophesy" to me. She told me that I would be successful when older (I was in my early twenties at the time) and have three children, a boy and two girls. When she talked about having three kids, I thought, *Absolutely not!* I paid her and left her table in a daze, meditating on what she had said. The woman she referred to later became my wife. We actually had three children, all girls, not one boy. The psychic was partially correct.

Like the damsel with the spirit of divination in Acts 16 I referenced earlier, this psychic's power was derived from a demonic source. The images on and use of tarot cards have been historically linked to witchcraft. At the time of my visit, I was ignorant of this. Please don't ever involve yourselves with psychics. You might open doors that are extremely hard to close. However, if you have done this, don't be discouraged. Renounce your involvement with these psychics and ask the Lord to release your prophetic gifting in a fuller and stronger measure.

Prophets are not psychics. There's a major difference. Many false or presumptuous prophets have caused some to seek out psychics due to the consistent inaccuracies of their utterances. Whenever true prophecy is spoken, it births revelation within the recipient. Prophets and prophetic people have the gift of receiving revelation. Psychics pick up words from the air. In fact, Ephesians 2:2 calls the devil *"the prince of the power of the air."* Prophets receive their words from God, not the air. Words can be jumbled by the wind, so whenever words are transported by air, they tend to be wrong. We must understand here that there are two separate and main sources of power in the world—the power of good and evil.

According to First Corinthians 14:3, the end result of all prophecy is edification, exhortation, and comfort. The final outcome of psychic consultation is ultimately devastation, discouragement, and discomfort. The devil will counterfeit and distort the word of Lord, filling it with errors and lies. The psychic simply regurgitates these falsehoods mixed with truth to God's people like Satan did to Eve in the Garden of Eden (see Gen. 3:1-13). All prophets are seers, but they do more than just see. They see and address issues in your life, and psychics will not. Many times, we want prophets to deal with the ongoing problems in our lives and tell us how to remove them. Psychics don't normally do that. They only do what the amount of money given dictates. Prophets can't tell you everything about your future, only what God releases them to say. They're not here to predict your future but to say what God says.

Psychics commonly charge you for a word pertaining to your future. True prophets of God will not charge for a word that comes from Him. If anyone ever attempts to charge you for a prophetic word, *run*. It's not of God. The story of Simon the sorcerer applies here.

> *And when Simon saw that through laying on of the apostles' hands the Holy Ghost was given, he offered them money, Saying, Give me also this power, that on whomsoever I lay hands, he may receive the Holy Ghost. But Peter said unto him, Thy money perish with thee, because thou hast thought that the gift of God may be purchased with money. Thou hast neither*

part nor lot in this matter: for thy heart is not right in the sight of God (Acts 8:18-21).

If you peruse this chapter, you'll find that Simon considered himself a great man. He practiced magic arts and was able to perform many wondrous acts. This was before Phillip came along and demonstrated the incredible, awesome power of the Holy Spirit. Simon's "magic" was no match for the *dunamis* (power) of God. Simon believed as well even to the point of baptism. However, I believe that he had ulterior motives for getting saved. He wanted the power, but not the King. This is demonstrated in Acts 8:15-21 when Peter and John came down to pray for the Samaritans and laid hands upon them so that they received the Holy Spirit. Simon saw this and offered them money for their gift (see Acts 8:18). He wanted the power and authority that he saw demonstrated, including the ability to lay hands on others and impart the Holy Spirit. Peter rebuked him sharply, speaking destruction to Simon and his money. He emphasized that the gift of God was free. That's the focus of this particular passage of Scripture. The prophetic gift is not for sale. Peter let Simon know that his heart was wrong. Those that charge money for prophetic words are acting as psychics not as prophets. Simon asked John and Peter to pray for him that none of the sharp words of impending destruction would befall him. He seemed to see the error of his ways and was essentially sorry. This spirit of currency has tried to attach itself to many a prophet and, in some cases, has succeeded. Such heinous acts misrepresent and grieve the Holy Spirit. Jesus never charged anyone for healing them. He never made the disciples pay for instructing them. Some people routinely charge for their experience and revelation. They should realize that they only have both because of God.

Matthew 10:7-8 tells us, *"And as ye go, preach, saying, The kingdom of heaven is at hand. Heal the sick, cleanse the lepers, raise the dead, cast out devils: freely ye have received, freely give."* Freely you have received, freely give. This statement is a Kingdom concept. It's the way of our Lord. Psychics are more concerned about merchandising than ministering. They have no power to change for the better but can only see by demonic intuition. Please understand that although a gift comes from God, a person might use it for evil purposes. If you look at the world today, you see many gifted singers, actors, and dancers. They were given their talent to honor God. He will not take these gifts away even when we misuse them. However, our gifts might become tainted by dirty oil, which is the anointing or effectiveness of the gift in the long run. I've seen many talented people meet an early death possibly because they compromised their gifts by not using them for the glory of God. Some psychics fall into this same category. They were mandated by the Lord to use their gifts for the Kingdom but chose to use them to make money.

Psychics and Prophets Are Not the Same

Godly prophets have the following qualities:

- Humility

- Solid character

- Purity

- Holiness

- Not money-oriented

Psychics are just the opposite and operate out of demonic or familiar spirits. They're soothsayers or diviners. Balaam was a soothsayer. The psychic realm is real and includes Ouija boards, crystal balls, tea leaves, etc. The root problem is rebellion. Scripture lets us know that rebellion is as the sin of witchcraft (see 1 Sam. 15:23). False religions have false prophets as described in Matthew 24:11.

Psychics believe in luck while true prophets believe in God. He is their source, not chance. The Lord's Kingdom does not have bad or good luck. However, prophets of God know how to look at difficult situations and people and pull out the gold of their potential for God's glory.

CHAPTER 17

The Toxic Tongue

But the tongue can no man tame; it is an
unruly evil, full of deadly poison (James 3:8).

Too many times, I've read and heard prophecies that reek of two stubborn spirits—rejection and offense. The words birthed from these two spirits have a tendency to promote strife and dissension. Don't allow your prophetic utterances to be tainted by rejection or offense. Words from the Lord can be infected by ill feelings toward the recipient. For example, if you have had a huge argument with someone, you should definitely not minister to them. You must first reconcile your differences before imparting healing words from the Lord your God.

If you have an offense against someone, don't speak the word of the Lord to them until you make things right with the person and God. Make sure that you are free from all unforgiveness before ministering to them so that your words will produce life instead of your tongue releasing toxic poisons. There aren't too many things worse than receiving a polluted prophetic word from someone who doesn't like you. Am I saying that you can never speak a word to someone you dislike? No, but I am saying that you should seek to address any unresolved issues between you and that person if at all possible. It takes a certain level of maturity to go to a person who has offended you, rather than going to everyone else but the offender. Matthew 18:15 addresses this in no uncertain terms. *"Moreover if thy brother shall trespass against thee, go and tell him his fault between thee and him alone: if he shall hear thee, thou hast gained thy brother."*

In order to keep your prophetic stream pure, you must guard your heart. You have to diligently keep it from being infected with bitterness due perceived and real offenses. You can do this by keeping your focus on the Lord and not on what others are doing to you. If wounded by someone, forgive them immediately. Remember, forgiveness is a state not a feeling. You must first confess forgiveness regularly, and the feelings will come later. This helps to stop the root of bitterness from growing in you before it starts. The spirit of offense is alive and well in the church today. This heinous spirit has had a stronghold over people since the church's inception. When you operate from a spirit of offense, almost anything will upset you. Refuse to give into this spirit.

"Behold, I give unto you power to tread on serpents and scorpions, and over all the power of the enemy: and nothing shall by any

means hurt you" (Luke 10:19). This Scripture affirms that Jesus Christ gave us *dunamis* and *exousia* to tread on serpents and scorpions and over *all* the power of the enemy. You have the power and authority in Jesus' Name to overcome varying levels of offense. Don't let this spirit control your attitude, emotions, or actions. Don't allow it to taint the prophetic words that you release. This nefarious demon can fester in people for years before manifesting as bitterness and rejection. Anger is its constant companion and will come to its aid when necessary. Don't allow the spirit of offense to infect your body. Once caught, it's very contagious.

Part IV

THE PROPHETIC CHURCH

CHAPTER 18

Not-for-Prophet Churches

And whosoever shall not receive you, nor hear
your words, when ye depart out of that house or
city, shake off the dust of your feet. Verily I say
unto you, It shall be more tolerable for the land
of Sodom and Gomorrha in the day of judgment,
than for that city (Matthew 10:14-15).

A couple of years ago, I was at a Sunday worship service at Crusaders Church in Chicago, Illinois. The anointing was high with amazing worship. Apostle John Eckhardt made a powerful statement during his message that has stayed with me until this very day. He stated that there are some "not-for-prophet churches" in existence today. I thought it was hilarious at the time, but in retrospect, it's also very sad. How can any church of our Lord Jesus Christ not be prophetic? Scripture informs us in Revelation 19:10 that the very testimony of Jesus Christ is the spirit of prophecy. The Old Testament is filled with prophecies about Him. In fact, most of the books in the Old Testament were written by prophets. We cannot get around the massive evidence of prophetic influence throughout the holy Word of God.

My definition of a "not-for-prophet" church is one that's not for prophets. A visual image of such an edifice is one in which prophetic people are in the middle of a vast ocean and the senior leader is on the shore, shouting directions that can't be heard due to the distance. A gulf or chasm exists between prophetic desire and prophetic instruction within these churches. I've met many who were in or are still in these types of churches. These people are called to be prophets or are interested in the prophetic but are "stuck" in a not-for-prophet church. They go to "First Thessalonians Monumental Missionary Church" pastored by Ebenezer Scrooge the Second, and he has no intention of allowing prophecy to illuminate his darkened ministry. When I meet such people, I wonder why they are there. Their answers vary from "My family goes there" to "I'm afraid to leave." Please understand that I don't advise anyone to leave a church unless there's clear evidence of abusive practices within leadership, but I'll never understand how anyone can stay somewhere that does not further the calling of God upon their lives.

As I said in Chapter 14, I've seen pastoral candidates languish in ministries for twenty-plus years, never receiving any formal training pertaining to their mandate. It is illogical and unreasonable for those with a growing desire to flow in their prophetic gifts to remain in an "un-prophetic" church. I've witnessed those with tremendous calls upon their lives drown in institutions that refused to allow them to swim. Like the prophetic people in the middle of the lake, they're so far away from the leader that they can't hear him or her, and he or she can't hear them. In many cases, this is a communication issue within these churches. The leaders are not hearing the prophets, and the prophets aren't really hearing the leaders. Both remain in a limbo of sorts, coexisting without comingling in terms of prophetic connection.

If the leader (head) is not prophetic, the church (Body) never will be. I know this statement to be true through personal experience. I have seen people in a church claim that they were called to go to another ministry in order to usher in the prophetic. This usually turns into an exercise in futility if the head is not prophetic. Most of the time, this "mandate" is a fruitless endeavor, resulting in frustration due to the unwillingness of the leader to receive what the person feels God instructed them to share. What's in the church leader will be evident within the congregation. For example, if the pastor is loving, then most of the congregants will be as well. If the leader doesn't display a loving nature, then most of the membership will not either. Everything flows down from the top, not up. Psalm 133:2 provides an illustration of this principle. *"It is like the precious ointment upon the head, that ran down the beard, even Aaron's beard: that went down to the skirts of his garment."*

This Scripture represents the anointing (effectiveness) flowing from the top down, not from the bottom up. Many in the Body (the bottom) mistakenly believe that their assignment is to tell church leadership (the top) how to run the congregation. This is out of order. In a grocery store, the cashier doesn't tell the manager what to do. It's quite the opposite due to their given roles. I'm not saying that a leader cannot receive counsel or suggestions from those in the pews, but I am saying that orders should not come from them. I've seen church members use "God said" as a tool of manipulation. In essence, they will tell the leader that the Lord gave them specific instructions on how to run the church. The leader has no idea what they are talking about. Worse yet, he or she might feel that they need to take the church in a completely different direction.

During the early years of my pastoral ministry, a Jezebel came to our ministry and told me that "God said" unless I wore a robe every time I preached, the church would fail. I didn't receive it and politely told her that I only wear robes during weddings and funerals. She reacted negatively and left our ministry a short time later. She and countless others have used "thus saith the Lord" to control and manipulate people. I've learned to challenge "God said" believers with "No, God didn't say." I don't believe that most mean any harm. They just want their voices to be heard. In most cases, using this phrase amplifies their sound. They think it will command attention and obedience, but if you don't feel it's God, you don't have to obey.

In my travels, few things bother me more than un-prophetic churches or "not-for-prophet" organizations. I have never understood how some churches simply adhere to a few of the nine gifts of the Spirit and ignore the rest. When dealing with Scripture, we're to eat the whole scroll not just the portions that "taste good." If you feel that God called you to be a prophet or have a high interest in the prophetic, you need to be in an environment conducive to spiritual growth in that area. From the worship to the Word, the prophetic should be evident. If prophecy is not flowing from the head, it will be extremely difficult for it to emerge from the Body. I'm not saying that the church should overdose on the prophetic; balance is definitely a godly characteristic. Too many times, people overly emphasize the prophetic and fail to apply and walk out what they have learned. Proverbs 11:1 gives us further clarification. *"A false balance is an abomination to the Lord, but a just weight is His delight."*

This balance should be consistently seen in the local church. In the apostolic church, it should be a crime if prophecy is banned or if the apostle cannot prophesy. Today's church should have a prophetic dimension and anointing if we ever want to fulfill the mandate of God. How then can we omit a gift as precious as prophecy? Prophecy has the power to augment or alter the very course of your life. I have seen this personally. Selah!

Having a prophet speak at a church does not necessarily make that church prophetic. Some think that if they have "master prophet chicken wing" minister at their church enough times, they will magically become prophetic. While they might become a bit prophetic for the three hours that he's there each year, they will go back to their old ways each time he leaves. If they want lasting change, they will need to implement ongoing training, activation, education, and impartation. If not, then that particular house is not prophetic. I've seen many churches prophesy, but they aren't necessarily prophetic. In other words, some "non-prophetic" churches use prophecy because they've witnessed others do it. They don't really believe in it, instruct others in it, or make it an integral part of their DNA. As I mentioned in Chapter 3 regarding the seven sons of Sceva in Acts 19:13-16, these men did not have an intimate or seasoned relationship with Christ. A church that is void of a prophetic dimension is subject to demonic infiltration. These churches don't have watchmen on duty, or if they do, the watchmen are asleep on the job. Prophets are watchmen who protect the house. We are instructed by God in Isaiah 21:6 to set a watchmen over His house to say what He sees. *"For thus hath the Lord said unto me, Go, set a watchman, let him declare what he seeth."*

Not-for-prophet churches are at an enormous disadvantage here. If there is no watchman or prophet, then witches and/or warlocks might sneak in and wreak havoc. They're especially attracted to apostolic and prophetic churches but have a harder time sneaking in due to the seers who continuously keep watch. However, an establishment that maintains a pseudo-prophetic presence is ripe for an invasion. *Pseudo* means false, feigned, erroneous, in appearance only, or resembling. These churches resemble a prophetic house on the outside, but inside they're full of dead men's bones. I say that because the prophetic brings life to a church not death. In fact, not just life, but light. It illuminates ministries which have been darkened through religious routines that avoid anything that goes against traditional practices. Many don't embrace the prophetic due to fear of it. We need proper instruction in order to demystify prophetic ministry. Much of the prophetic in these churches is for display instead of demonstration. It's visible but not experienced. The only time prophecy goes forth within the ministry is seasonal and only from the pastor and their spouse. No other voices are allowed to speak what God has given to them for the church. Usually, this is a sign of unnatural and ungodly control. We're told not to be lords over God's heritage in First Peter 5:3 but to lead by example.

As a leader of a prophetic church, I should be able to produce a prophetic people. A carbon copy will never be as great or as valuable as an original. Leaders should not create clones, but whatever you are in God should be evident in those who follow you as you follow Christ. As a prophet, I should produce originals not echoes. My prophetic anointing should be evident in the sons and daughters who are birthed from my ministry. I don't try to influence how they prophesy, just how well they hear God. I teach them to *know* His voice. That way, 100 percent prophetic accuracy won't be a problem. Am I saying that prophets never miss it? Absolutely not! If one doesn't hear from God, inaccurate words will result. This happens frequently in churches that don't know God prophetically. If they did, they would know Him as the God of prophecy. His very nature is prophetic. If His nature is prophetic, His churches should be as well.

I'm both amazed and bewildered by some of my colleagues' aversion to anything that relates to prophecy. The churches they govern skip over it as if it were evil. When it comes to Scripture, we take the Word of God as a whole, not just pick and choose the parts that we like or dislike. You can see this type of behavior in many not-for-prophet churches.

Churches Without a Prophetic Advantage

I've ministered prophetically in many places over the years and have a pretty solid track record for prophetic accuracy. I've been in far too many churches with no idea of how the prophetic works. In one case, I spoke a word to someone, and their relative became upset about what I said. They told the host pastor who then called me, questioning the prophecy. I told him that I had to be obedient to God. Furthermore, the people need to be trained in the area of prophecy. They should know how to war over the words received instead of fearing them. This incident is a clear example that some words from the Lord might bring correction instead of tickling your flesh.

True Prophetic Houses

We are of God: he that knoweth God
heareth us; he that is not of God heareth
not us. Hereby know we the spirit of truth,
and the spirit of error. (1 John 4:6)

The prophetic ministry should be a normal
part of the ministry of the local church.[1]

When in a prophetic church, you might become "accidently" prophetic. Remember, this happened to Saul in First Samuel 10. He prophesied when he was around a company of prophets. Prophetic churches have more than one prophet in their congregation. These churches have established and operational prophetic presbyteries or teams. Prophecy is not exclusive to the husband and wife who lead the church but inclusive of the prophetic presbytery within the church. I have heard many stories of churches like these where there is no liberty for these gifted people to declare the word of the Lord. I'm not saying that ministries should have prophetic free-for-alls. I am saying that proper training, processing, and commissioning should occur within the church. Once trained, prophetic teams should be established to speak during and after the service to exhort, edify, and comfort the Body. This not only helps the place of worship, but it takes much of the weight off the leaders when you can employ trusted voices to deliver the word of the Lord. It must be a team effort instead of a one-man show. I truly believe that liberty is one of the hallmarks of a ministry that operates strongly in the prophetic. We see this in Second Corinthians 3:17. *"Now the Lord is that Spirit: and where the Spirit of the Lord is, there is liberty."*

The Spirit of the Lord is present in true prophetic churches. Jesus was prophesied about long before His birth. His arrival was the fulfillment of all the prophetic words spoken in the Old Testament. All that our Lord went through for us comprises His testimony. Not only was His coming prophetic, but His Spirit was as well. If His Spirit dwells within a church, so should prophecy. If His Spirit dwells in us personally, so should prophecy. To say that you're a Christian but to not be prophetic in any way is a denial of the true nature of Christ. He was prophetic on purpose, for purpose, and so should we be. His testimony is the basis for many church services throughout the world. This should especially be true in ministries that believe in the nine gifts of the Spirit and that operate in the fivefold gifts. Please use the list and Scriptures below as a reference.

The Nine Gifts of the Spirit
(First Corinthians 12:1, 8-11)

1. Word of Wisdom

2. Word of Knowledge

3. Discernment of Spirits

4. Prophecy

5. Divers Kinds of Tongues

6. The Interpretation of Tongues

7. The Gift of Faith

8. The Gift of Healing

9. The Gift of Miracles

The Gift Ministries/FiveFold
(Ephesians 4:11)

1. Apostles

2. Prophets

3. Evangelists

4. Pastors

5. Teachers

Prophetic Activations

Prophetic churches *want* to activate people. Based on first-hand experience, prophetic activations work! The foundation for this is Second Timothy 1:6. Paul wrote the following to Timothy: *"Wherefore I put thee in remembrance that thou stir up the gift of God, which is in thee by the putting on of my hands."* Here, the apostle Paul was admonishing his spiritual son, Timothy, to stir up or activate the gift of God that was given him by the laying on of his spiritual father's hands. Notice that Paul didn't ask Timothy to ask the Lord to shake up the gift. He told Timothy to do this himself. He basically wanted Timothy to stir up what was already inside of him. Father God still wants us to do the same today.

Activation means to make active or more active. When someone is activated prophetically, the gift within them is stirred up. When one gift is activated, other gifts might be shaken, moved, and stirred as a result. This means that as one present is unwrapped, other gifts around it seem to be unwrapped as well. In some of my prophetic activation services, the healing gifts manifested as prophetic gifts were stirred up. I receive testimony after testimony concerning the validity of said trainings, which convinces me even further how much they are needed across the Body of Christ. The time of church as just a spectator sport is over. The time for just listening to a message and going home after church is over. We must be active participants in shaping our gifts and ministries. We need to be stirred to action not apathetic when it comes to our God-given mandates. This is what prophetic activations do.

Recently, I experienced something that I'd never seen before during a prophetic activation—two individuals began manifesting demons. We were in the middle of the service, and two people began crying out. Our deliverance team immediately ministered to them, and they were set free. I believe that this happened due to the tangible presence of the Holy Spirit within the room. Where the Spirit of the Lord is, the enemy will manifest. Whenever your gift is activated, the devil will start to chime in. He will begin to attack due to the fear that he experiences when your gifts are stirred up. The enemy literally and figuratively bears witness to your future. He knows that when your gifts are activated, you become a major threat to his kingdom.

Most of the prophets and prophetic people I know experienced severe complications at birth. As you read in the introductory chapter of this book, so did I. These similar occurrences among seers led me to the conclusion that Satan attempts to prevent God's oracles from seeing by killing them before they mature. In my own life, Lucifer laid many traps meant to cause my demise, but God wouldn't allow them to succeed. He protected me each and every time. Hallelujah!

What I've written thus far is not exhaustive by any means in regard to this subject. I just wanted to give you a quick overview. For more information and revelation on this subject, I highly recommend that you purchase the book *Prophetic Activation* by Apostle John Eckhardt.

Note

1. John Eckhardt, *A Shift in Leadership: Transitioning from the Pastoral to the Apostolic*, (Olympia Fields, IL: John Eckhardt Ministries, 2015).

Part V

RESOURCES

CHAPTER 20

Confessions, Prayers, and Prophetic Words

Daily Confessions for the Supernaturally Prophetic

- I speak as an oracle of God (1 Peter 4:11).

- I hear Him clearly (Revelation 3:22).

- I know Him intimately (John 10:14).

- I listen when He speaks (Deuteronomy 28:1-2).

- I am attentive to His words (Isaiah 55:3).

- I walk in the wisdom of heaven (James 3:17).

- I am His messenger (Isaiah 6:8).

- I speak the truth in love (Ephesians 4:15).

- I reject my own will (John 4:34).

- I embrace His will (Luke 22:42).

- I am His mouthpiece (Exodus 4:16).

- I make His mind audible to others (1 Corinthians 2:16).

- I give words that express His heart (Acts 13:22).

- I edify others through His words (Ephesians 4:29).

- I exhort others through His words (1 Corinthians 14:3).

- I comfort others with His words (1 Thessalonians 5:11).

- I am His prophet (2 Chronicles 20:20).

- I say what He says (Isaiah 38:5).

Activation Prayer for Prophetic People

Father God, I pray that every believer will realize their full prophetic potential while they are yet in the realm of the living. They will actualize the gifts that reside in each and every one of them. They will come into full knowledge that prophecy is the divine right of every single Holy-Ghost-filled believer. From all over the world, they will be stirred up to speak what "thus saith the Lord!" And from out of these individuals will come words from God that will change the course of neighborhoods, cities, states, and countries! Fear will no longer clamp their mouths shut. In fact, fear will cause them to cry louder and spare not. I pray that boldness will come upon your prophetic soldiers and that they will say what you say without compromise. Father, allow their spiritual hearing to be sharper, their vision keener, and their discernment clearer. I come against the spirit of error. I pray that consistent fallacy will not be found among them but that they will walk in authenticity, accuracy, and exactness. Lord, I petition you to sound the alarm within your prophetic people! Give them a mindset to be trained, activated, and educated in the realm of the prophetic. We come against the spirit of arrogance that seeks to dilute spiritual understanding with the satisfaction of the flesh. Let not the carnal mind overtake the spirit of prophecy that lives inside every believer. As Jesus Christ abides in the body of every Holy-Spirit-filled person, so resides the spirit of prophecy. Let the Spirit of Christ empower prophetic people in this hour. Push them, oh God, to greater dimensions in you and allow them platforms to speak your word! Father God, I pray that they will emerge as never before, having the spirit of Macaiah to speak the truth regardless of the consequences and without fear. I pray all this in the Name of the Lord Jesus Christ.

Identity Prayer for Prophetic People

Father God, I pray for each person who does not know his/her position in you to supernaturally hear your directives for their lives. Lord, make their position in the Body of Christ crystal clear to them. Help them to make their calling and election sure. Remove every doubt that would try to persuade them not to believe your spoken words. Please allow signs and miracles to follow your people as they follow Christ. Give them clarity in their calling. Let all their physical senses line up in agreement with the mandate you've placed upon their lives. Release continuous confirmations of their identities in abundance. Reset their thinking about who they are called to be. Do not permit any strategy of Satan to derail their knowledge of who they are in you. I come against every destiny blocker and loose destiny enhancers into their lives. I decree that they will know their calling, gifts, and purpose in you as never before! I come against the spirits of fear, offense, apathy, laziness, complacency, oppression, depression, anxiety, rejection, and every other demonic force that attempts to blind them to what God truly has in store for their lives, in the matchless Name of Jesus Christ.

Personal Prayer for the Emerging Prophet

Lord, I come to you as a person pregnant with prophetic promise. Like Timothy, I, (your name here), ask you to show me how to stir up the gift that I've had since birth. Father, please give me an unobscured view of my Kingdom assignment. Let me know exactly who I am in you so that doubt, fear, and insecurity will have no place in me. Father God, give me the strength to incline my ears to your wisdom and release that same wisdom to your people. Increase the word of wisdom within me so that I might guide others in the way you would have them go. Augment the word of knowledge within me to show your people where they've been. Strengthen the gift of prophecy in me so that I can show others their future in you. Father, allow all my gifts to emerge in this season for the benefit of the Body. Whatever gifts are in me beyond the prophetic, let them emerge. Any of the nine gifts of the Spirit that make their home in me, be released now! I come against any strongholds of phobia, self-doubt, unbelief, mistrust, apprehension, disillusionment, mystification, nervousness, paranoia, misgivings, apathy, neglect, misuse, ignorance, indifference, and laziness that have kept me from operating fully in the gifts God has given me. I pray and decree all of the above in the mighty Name of Jesus Christ.

Prophetic Words

Run, Prophet, Run!

Merowts, a Hebrew word pronounced *May-rotes*, means "a run (trial of speed) or race" (Strong's #H4793). Your current condition is not your conclusion. Your book has not been finished yet. You're just dealing with an unruly chapter in your life. This, too, shall pass. Endurance is your portion during this season. God has bestowed upon you the spirit of a long-distance runner. With this spirit, endurance trumps speed. Sometimes you want to speed up when the Lord is telling to slow down. You are consistently gaining ground through every heartache, misstep, and setback. Remember, the race is not for the swift, nor the battle for the strong (see Eccles. 9:11). You need endurance so that after you have done the will of God, you can receive what He's promised you (see Heb. 10:36). This is your time to complete the *merowts* (race) that God has placed before you. No matter what obstacles stand in your way, God has given you the ability to leap over them and continue to run, gain ground, and finish your race. I speak and decree a finisher's anointing on you. You will complete that which God has begun in you (see Phil. 1:6).

Word of Advice to Emerging Prophets

As God elevates you, always guard yourself against the spirit of pride and arrogance. They work in tandem with the intent to destroy you from the inside out. Conceit should never be found in or around the prophetic. Pride can actually be built up in you through continued success as you use your gift. We must always be on high alert when it comes to this because it's the same spirit that caused Lucifer to be kicked out of heaven as described in Ezekiel 28 and Isaiah 14. You must never, ever allow your gift to own you. On the contrary, your gift was given to you by God. You steward it during your time here on earth. In fact, you're not just the owner but the manager as well. The Lord gives us gifts to use to complete our divine assignments in the Earth realm. Never allow pride in your ability to cause you to miss the will of the Most High. Those who have done so suffered a major fall. Look to the fate of Lucifer when feelings of arrogance try to overwhelm you. Address them, repent, and move forward in your calling. This will help you to become supernaturally prophetic.

About Dr. John Veal

D r. John Veal is the senior pastor/prophet of Enduring Faith Christian Center and the CEO of John Veal Ministries. He is passionate about pursuing God's mandate to preach, teach, impart, and activate people within the prophetic. Dr. Veal is a highly sought-after conference speaker due to his uncanny prophetic accuracy, humor, candor, and unconventional preaching style. He has traveled the nations, presenting a myriad of prophetic training and ministry. He currently resides in Chicago, Illinois, with his wife, Elisa, and their three children.

I'd love to hear from you!

If you would like to learn more about my ministry or contact me, you may visit my website at www.johnveal.org. You can keep up with my schedule and find out where I will be speaking. For booking information, please visit www.johnveal.org/bookings/.

I pastor a local church in the Chicago area:

> Enduring Faith Christian Center
> P.O. Box 19536
> Chicago, IL 60619
> The church website is www.faith2endure.com.

If you have enjoyed this book, please write a review on Amazon. You can also find out more information about it by visiting www.supernaturallyprophetic.com or by contacting us at supernaturallyprophetic@gmail.com.

Thank you so much, and God bless you.

Follow Me Online

Facebook: https://www.facebook.com/prophetjv/

On Twitter: @pastorveal

On Instagram: www.Instagram.com/prophetjohnveal